A READER IN CONTEMPORARY THEOLOGY

A Reader in Contemporary Theology

Edited by
JOHN BOWDEN
and
JAMES RICHMOND

SCM PRESS LTD

334 01366 6

First published 1967
by SCM Press Ltd
56 Bloomsbury Street London WC1
Second, Revised Edition 1971

Printed in Great Britain by
Fletcher & Son Ltd
Norwich

CONTENTS

ACKNOWLEDGEMENTS

THE EDITORS thank the publishers and individuals for permission to reprint material included in this book which originally appeared as follows:

Karl Barth, 'The Christian Understanding of Revelation', in Karl Barth, *Against the Stream: Shorter Post-War Writings 1946–52*, SCM Press, 1954, pp. 205–12, 214.

Rudolf Bultmann, 'Jesus Christ and Mythology', in Rudolf Bultmann, *Jesus Christ and Mythology*, SCM Press, 1960, pp. 15–18, 35f., 43, 45f., 48–56, 60, 68–71.

Paul Tillich, 'The Divine Name', in Paul Tillich, *The Eternal Now*, SCM Press, 1963, pp. 77–84; permission for Canada granted by Charles Scribner's Sons, New York. 'Martin Buber', in *Pastoral Psychology*, September 1965, pp. 52–4, 66, reprinted by permission of Professor Robert C. Kimball, Literary Executor for the Estate of Paul Tillich.

Karl Rahner, 'God', 'Jesus Christ', 'Nature and Grace', 'Philosophy and Theology', articles in Karl Rahner, Herbert Vorgrimler, *Concise Theological Dictionary*, Burns and Oates, 1965, pp. 186–9, 238–42, 308f., 355–8.

Eduard Schillebeeckx, 'The Sacraments, An Encounter with God', in Daniel J. Callahan, Heiko A. Oberman, Daniel J. O'Hanlon (eds.), *Christianity Divided*, Sheed and Ward, 1962, pp. 245–54, 268–70.

Pierre Teilhard de Chardin, 'The Essence of the Phenomenon of Man', in Pierre Teilhard de Chardin, *The Phenomenon of Man*, Fontana Books, 1965, pp. 328–36.

C. F. von Weizsäcker, 'What is Secularization?' in C. F. von Weizsäcker, *The Relevance of Science. Creation and Cosmogony*, Gifford Lectures, 1959–60, Collins, 1964, pp. 160–70, 178–81.

Dietrich Bonhoeffer, 'The Non-religious Interpretation of Biblical Concepts', in Dietrich Bonhoeffer, *Letters and Papers from Prison*, rev. ed., SCM Press, 1967, pp. 152ff., 178ff., 195ff.

Cornelis van Peursen, 'Man and Reality – The History of Human Thought', in *The Student World*, lvi, 1963, no. 1, pp. 13–21. Reprinted by permission of the World Student Christian Federation.

R. B. Braithwaite, *An Empiricist's View of the Nature of Religious Belief*, Eddington Memorial Lecture, Cambridge University Press, 1955, pp. 2–11, 18–28, 30–5.

John Wisdom, 'The Garden', in John Wisdom, 'Gods', *Proceedings of the Aristotelian Society 1944–45*, pp. 191–3, reprinted by permission of the Editor of the Aristotelian Society.

Basil Mitchell, 'The Stranger', in Antony Flew and Alasdair MacIntyre (eds.), *New Essays in Philosophical Theology*, SCM Press, 1955, pp. 103f.

John Hick, 'The Road', in John Hick, *Philosophy of Religion*, Prentice-Hall, 1963, pp. 101f., © 1963. Reprinted by permission of Prentice-Hall, Inc., Englewood Cliffs, New Jersey, USA.

H. D. Lewis, 'The Limits and Lessons of Empiricism', in H. D. Lewis, *The Philosophy of Religion*, English Universities Press, 1965, pp. 131–9.

David Jenkins, 'Whither the Doctrine of God Now?', in *The London Quarterly and Holborn Review*, July 1964, pp. 198–205. Reprinted by permission of Epworth Press.

John Macquarrie, 'The Service of Theology', in John Macquarrie, *Studies in Christian Existentialism*, SCM Press, 1966, pp. 19–28.

PREFACE

THIS *Reader* has been planned as a sketch map of contemporary theology. It is not meant to stand on its own or to illuminate the whole range of theology, but to illustrate several issues which seem to be particularly important today. As in other subjects, the beginner may find it best to take up one of the themes (or groups of themes) highlighted here and to follow it through with a programme of organized reading, however modest; the selected texts and the brief comments on them should serve as bearings to steer by in the course of exploration.

When the first edition appeared in 1967, one reviewer picked on another analogy to illustrate the purpose of the *Reader*. He compared it to the 'sampler' records issued by the major record companies to tempt listeners on to music they might not otherwise hear by grouping together on one disc extracts from larger-scale recordings: 'The World of the Academy of St Martin in the Fields', 'The Golden Ring', 'The Enjoyment of Music', 'The World of Joan Sutherland'. The purchaser pays a modest price and then finds himself irretrievably attracted into spending much more to enlarge his repertoire. That is about it. While it would be perhaps over-optimistic to expect that theology could out-charm music (one editor has to confess that his last new penny would have to go on the latter), we still feel that if the reader is not led to buy at least one more book of theology before he reaches the final pages, then we (and, indeed, contemporary theology) have failed in our task. Hence the copious references to other literature which in places make the book resemble a publisher's catalogue.

So here is something of 'The World of Modern Theology'. Before we enter it, however, there is some explanation to be done.

The texts included here were chosen during the summer of 1966, and the *Reader* was first published in 1967. Four years have gone by since then, and yet the same collection is presented again in a slightly larger format, unchanged apart from a new Preface and Postscript and a few alterations in the introductory material, particularly to bring the bibliographies up to date. Is this fair? Have there not been considerable changes in the theological world, as elsewhere, in the interval? Ought not a map or sampler to have changed with the times? Should it not introduce the newest thinking that has emerged?

There are several (we think) good reasons for keeping the *Reader* basically as it was. There is, of course, the economic one. Publishing books is 'labour intensive', and costs have spiralled dramatically in the present inflation. A much longer *Reader*, or even a much-changed *Reader*, would have had to be priced out of the range of the audience for which it is intended. In any case, over the past four years the compiling of anthologies has multiplied, particularly in the higher price-ranges. The *Reader* was one of the first of its kind to appear; it was relatively short and inexpensive, and we are trying to keep as closely to the original idea as possible. (And please, if anyone is thinking of writing to the SCM Press to complain about the price of *this* book, do compare it with that of some of the other services and commodities around you, including sampler records, first.)

These comments on the economic facts of life, incidentally, illustrate a problem which looks as though it will become acute over the next decade. One of the most depressing features of the past five years has been the steady economic strangulation of religious journalism, affecting some of the periodicals which have done invaluable work either in producing the germs of new theology or interpreting difficult works to a wider audience. The effect of this pressure on book publishing has not been altogether unhealthy in that it has cleared away some of the undergrowth of theology; however, in the future, new growths are going to have to be much sturdier to survive the climate. Some of the most viable theology for the next decade will be found on the grapevine of study groups, lectures and occasional papers (see the Postscript) rather than in the commercial mushroom fields.

Publishing costs, however, are only one reason against change, and if they had been the only major one, changes would have been made. Looking at the *Reader* almost with new eyes and with four years more reading and experience, we were pleasantly surprised at how little *needed* to be changed. If one were to start choosing again, the ground plan might look different and some of the emphases would be changed. For example, Roman Catholic theology has yet to make the break-through that at one time seemed possible; the reviewer who remarked that the selections here represented the end of one chapter rather than the beginning of the next was quite right. But the principles behind the original selection do not seem to have been far out. The fundamental questions for theology, how to answer them and how not to answer them, are still to be seen in what follows.

What has changed is the context. A whole dimension seems to be missing from the original Preface. It was concerned almost exclusively with the practice of theology in purely theological questions. The main point that was made then was that a shift was taking place from 'biblical theology' to a theology involved with philosophy, psychology, sociology and other related disciplines, and indeed the whole of the *Reader* illustrates this shift. We wanted to show that the Bible was having a disproportionate amount of attention at the expense of other pressing religious questions which could not be dealt with solely in biblical terms. That point has now been taken – perhaps too well, to judge from the way in which some new school and university syllabuses are constructed. Now the argument has to be carried on in a different direction, against the question whether anything at all that is contained in this *Reader* has any relevance at all to the nineteen-seventies. The words which most excite and involve the more outspoken of the younger generation with religious concerns are 'freedom', 'revolution', 'racial equality', 'justice for the Third World', 'ecology', words relating to the social and international conditions and the environment in which we live. And one of the obvious things about the writers here is that most of them have very little to say on these issues, and that what they do say is often distressingly naive or over-intellectual. Why give them a hearing in a climate which seems – at least from the mass media – to be characterized increasingly by what a recent *Times Literary Supplement* survey called 'The Flight from Reason'?

> On all sides one hears or reads much the same stuff lauding the irrational, illogical and abnormal and ridiculing the rational, factual and normal. The treason of so many of our clerks (as it was between the wars) is greatest in its treachery to words, language, meanings, facts; whence of course it must bitterly assault history, the notion of objective science, logic, the principles and practice of scholarly learning, and the definitions of common terms in everyday discourse among children and adults.

The writer illustrates his thesis at length from a number of current books on economic history, and then comes to his own conclusion: 'Let the record stand. Many writers and teachers still write, teach, stand by, search for, eternal verities.'

What can be said by an economic historian in his field can surely be said by a theologian. Whatever the context, whatever the culture, whatever the fashion, if God is what the Christian tradition – and the Jewish tradition before that – has believed him to be, then certain questions about his nature and the possibility of human knowledge of him and recorded human experience of him will keep recurring. Unless reason is thrown overboard altogether and religious experience is totally divorced from social and ethical concern, looking for God in any form goes with a theology. It may be implicit or explicit, but it is there, and those who try to ignore the fact are usually not doing without theology altogether but implementing a bad theology.

A number of themes can be traced right across the book, as well as within the individual sections. One is the problem of what to make of the Bible – a disturbing feature of this small collection of theology is the wide discrepancy in the way in which the various writers make use of the Bible in their theology, which shows that we are still a long way from a satisfactory and agreed system of interpretation (the problem is taken up again in the Postscript). Another is the doctrine of God, a problem within which subsidiary questions can also be distinguished (compare, for example, the discussions of the name of God in the two Tillich extracts, van Peursen and Bonhoeffer). And one all-important question stands over the whole of theology, and underlies every single passage here until it is discussed thoroughly in the closing section. That is the question, 'How do you know?', the question that confronts every theologian whenever he thinks or speaks or writes. In our present context it also confronts everyone with any association with the Christian tradition in a slightly different form: 'What is it that you contribute to any of the discussions, actions, relationships in which you are involved as one who at least takes into account the possibility of God's being? What difference does it make?'

There were obvious omissions in the first edition besides the one already mentioned. There is nothing here about the vexed question of the relationship of Christianity to history, perhaps the most confused area of contemporary theology. The question of the basis of ethical judgments is barely touched on. The problem of evil, which seems to be one of the main questions to trouble agnostics and humanists, is not represented. And so on. The list could be considerably extended.

The Postscript at the end of the *Reader* attempts to show what progress has been made in British theology in discussing the questions to which the last section is devoted. This may seem unduly chauvinistic, but despite the historical dominance of German theology and the great volume and intensity of American theological study, it seems to be English theologians who, often in the informal way mentioned earlier and in less learned-looking books, have caught on to the crucial issues and are really grappling with them.

The only two German theologians to have made an international reputation in theology after the generation of Barth and Bultmann and their senior pupils are Jürgen Moltmann and Wolfhart Pannenberg. Moltmann, now Professor of Theology at Tübingen, is best known for his *Theology of Hope* (SCM Press,

1967) which has the distinction of already being in its third English edition. Inspired by the work of the Marxist philosopher Ernst Bloch, it attempts to restore to Christian thinking a dimension of future expectation, of which Marxism makes so much, in contrast to its tendency to orientation on the past. Moltmann's ideas are taken further in *Hope and Planning* (SCM Press, 1971): whether his approach to biblical interpretation is legitimate is very debatable. Pannenberg is represented in English by *Jesus – God and Man* (SCM Press, 1968) and *Basic Questions in Theology* (SCM Press, 1970). His thought is influenced by Hegel rather than by Marx, and in his book on christology he tries to reinstate the nineteenth-century philosopher's ambitious interpretation of history in terms that the modern world can accept. Unfortunately, it seems that, like Hegel, he has undertaken to demonstrate the undemonstrable.

Various readers and reviewers have either complained about aspects of the selections or expressed delight at new discoveries; the lists under the two headings are almost the same – which must prove something. But the best comment was that by the reviewer who remarked, 'It must have been fun to do'. It was.

HISTORICAL INTRODUCTION

IT MUST be realized that theology is never done in a vacuum. It is obvious that the great theologians have worked within and out of their own ecclesiastical and theological traditions. Nevertheless, they have also worked under the influence of, or in sympathy with, or in reaction against, all kinds of contemporary influences, movements, interests, theories, emphases and insights.

It follows that any attempt to understand a given theologian (or theological viewpoint) apart from the influences operative in his particular situation must be essentially an erroneous and often a disastrous one. This historical introduction, and the introductions to the various sections of this book, are designed to provide the reader with just a minimum of background material apart from which the sections themselves must remain largely unintelligible.

Recent and contemporary theology has as its historical background the entire movement of Western thought which probably received its initial impetus from that intellectual awakening of Western man which is usually called the Renaissance. Central to this movement is the rise of modern scientific method which has had (and is still having) an incalculably huge effect on our modern society. As is well known, modern science had important immediate implications for theology as early as the beginning of the seventeenth century. For instance, 'the new astronomy', associated with the names of Copernicus, Kepler and Galileo, seriously undermined the traditional earth-centred (geocentric) cosmology of the West which for over a millennium had seemed singularly sympathetic to the Christian way of looking at man's life in the world. But the rise of modern science has had at least two far-reaching consequences, perhaps even more important for theology, which we must try to grasp.

The first is that whereas as late as the seventeenth century philosophers and men of science tended on the whole to regard theology as the helpmaid of science, supplying science with valuable, even indispensable, clues and insights, by the end of the eighteenth century it was no longer clear just how theology could inform the scientist, or in what way the scientist must, partly at least, be dependent upon the theologian for guidance, information or inspiration. It became increasingly clear to the scientist that firm loyalty to his own scientific categories alone helped him towards the discovery of further clues to the nature of the universe. In other words, science became autonomous, independent of theology. For theology, this has increasingly meant that a drastic re-thinking of its fundamental assumptions and methods has become a necessity now that when man desires a description and explanation of the world around him, he turns to the scientist before and above anyone else. This whole matter will be taken up and explored further in section 4 of this book, 'Science and Secularization'.

The second is that the startling fruitfulness of scientific method, and the exceptional clarity of its categories and concepts (as manifested first towards the end of the sixteenth century), quite naturally gave rise in the West to an immense admiration and profound respect for that method as a means of enlarging our knowledge about reality. This admiration and respect have had a deep and lasting influence upon modern philosophy. For when philosophers contrasted the clarity and certainty of scientific knowledge with the unclarity of and the apparent contradictions within other types of alleged knowledge, say, speculative or theological ones, they were forced to raise in the most radical way difficult questions about the sources and nature of all valid human knowledge as such. The questions raised have been, for example, How do we know? What are the sources of our knowledge? Can we attain to knowledge by means other than our senses? Can we draw a clear distinction between the things that we can know and those which we cannot? Is there a realm or dimension beyond or behind the natural world which can only be grasped by extraordinary non-sensory means?

These questions properly belong to a branch of philosophy called theory of knowledge (epistemology), and this branch of the subject has largely dominated discussion between Western thinkers, beginning with the German philosopher Kant in the second half of the eighteenth century. What kind of answers have been given to these questions? It is dangerous to generalize. Nevertheless, with many notable and celebrated exceptions, in the last century and a half secular thinkers have tended to answer in this way: Ultimately, the source of what may legitimately be called 'knowledge' is our sense-experience of things, phenomena and events in space and time; the attempt to show that there are other sources of knowledge and ways of knowing involves a claim that places almost insuperable obstacles in the way of those who would attempt publicly to demonstrate its truth; we ought clearly to distinguish between those things knowledge of which is publicly demonstrable and those things which, although we may speculate about them for an eternity, cannot apparently be known with clarity or with any degree of certainty; consequently, the claim that there is obviously a realm above, beyond or behind the physical world has come to be regarded as, to say the least of it, dubious in the extreme.

This theory of knowledge, which appeals so firmly to sense-experience, is called in technical language *empiricism*, and those who adhere to it *empiricists*. It is a theory which has attracted many in modern society and has won many distinguished defenders. While it has gained the position almost of philosophical orthodoxy in the Anglo-Saxon tradition (more so in England than in the United States), its appeal has not been confined to it. Sometimes an empiricist viewpoint is combined with the more or less dogmatic claim that all knowledge worthy of the name is attainable only by the methods of the sciences, and this claim is a *positivistic* one, committing those who make it to scientific *positivism*. Frequently the claim that we can gain knowledge of supersensible reality is rejected so vehemently that those rejecting it embrace philosophical *naturalism*, the claim that reality is exhaustively identifiable with the natural, physical world, which, it is insisted, can only be understood in terms of forces, factors and processes immanent in that world. Of course, even more extreme anti-theological positions can be adopted, such as *materialism*, the claim that ultimate reality is matter, and that all phenomena must be understood in terms of processes and qualities immanent within that matter.

At any rate, it is not perhaps going too far to say that in the Western world the climate of opinion, for good or ill, tends to be *empiricistic*, *positivistic* and *naturalistic*. These views and their implications appear to be accepted, critically or uncritically, by the majority in our contemporary world. Theologically, that means that it is no longer obvious to the great mass of our contemporaries that religion still has valid knowledge to offer; it is no longer obvious that the average Western man or woman is obliged to have a religious outlook upon life; it is no longer obvious that religious practices should be indulged in and religious attitudes adopted. In short, an extremely common attitude appears to be *agnosticism*; the agnostic doubts whether the religious believer's claim to knowledge of the ultimate nature and destiny of things could ever be vindicated, at least with anything approximately approaching the certainty and clarity which he has become accustomed to from the empirical sciences.

Of course, we must not paint too gloomy a picture. On the side of philosophy, many have swum against the stream and have protested loudly, not against science itself, but against the insidious tendencies they have perceived in scientism, in the idolization of scientific detachment and in the lust for scientific certainty (see the excerpt from the writings of C. F. von Weizsäcker in section 4). To be more precise, they have been thoroughly alarmed at the dangers of dehumanization inherent in scientism, and have tried, not without success, to show that much of our modern culture, despite its vast achievements in the fields of technical knowledge and organization, has become apathetic, and occasionally downright hostile, to human freedom and dignity, and to man in so far as he tries to pursue his destiny as a creature not only of flesh and blood but also of spirit. Of those philosophies which have championed the uniquely human, *existentialism* is one of the most notable, but not, of course, the only one. We shall investigate *existentialist* types of theology in section 2 below.

Nor, in the crisis of our modern Western civilization, have the churches and their theologians been idle. We dare not ignore the truth in the accusation that the churches have too often been insensitive to the challenges and insights of accumulating modern knowledge, and have tended to turn away in dismay and hostility from the sceptical questioning of the modern world, directing their energies inwards towards strengthening and perpetuating ways of thought and life which belong to earlier ages. Despite these very real failings, there have been in modern times a host of notable attempts to refashion and restate the message of the Christian gospel in the light of contemporary culture, philosophy and science. Probably the 'classical age' of such theologizing was the nineteenth century in Europe, when such philosophical theologians as Friedrich Schleiermacher (1768-1834) and Albrecht Ritschl (1822-89), fully cognizant of the implications for religion of the philosophy and science of their day, offered reformulations of the Christian Faith designed to draw attention sharply to the immense perennial relevance of that Faith for man's life at its fullest and most human. Even if we judge, as do some, that their attempts were in the last analysis failures, this does not release us from the obligation to study their motives, their methods and the content of their theologies. For example, without some knowledge of nineteenth-century theology we could not understand section 1 of this book, the 'Theology of the Word of God', because we would be in the dark about those types of theology against which Karl Barth and his disciples reacted so vigorously several generations ago. Again, unless we understood something of nineteenth-century religious thought, we should be in some difficulty in reading the works of Bultmann, Tillich and Buber (section 2 below), precisely because these twentieth-century thinkers look back with varying degrees of admiration and respect to the previous century, and try in different ways to perpetuate in their own work something of the spirit and many of the ideals and aims of their illustrious predecessors. Again, ignorance of nineteenth-century studies would cause us grave difficulties when we grappled, for example, with the pages written by Dietrich Bonhoeffer, just because he, when he was setting down his revolutionary thoughts about secularization and man's 'coming of age', had influential nineteenth-century thinkers in mind.

In brief, the structure of classical nineteenth-century continental theology was this: The major theologians of the period were vividly aware of the power and autonomy of the empirical sciences. They were clear how the structure and operation of physical nature were being progressively illumined and mastered by the purely scientific intellect. But they were firmly convinced that there was one crucial area of reality which could never be fully understood by the processes of scientific knowing alone – that was the area of man's unique and all-important inner life, the world of man's profoundest feelings, visions and awarenesses, his strongest and most enduring religious drives and aspirations. Here, it was contended, was theology's starting-point, man's inner life. Here was where the philosophical theologian must seek for his primary data. Whether in the study, the lecture-room or the pulpit, the theologian and pastor must convey to their contemporaries that the Christian gospel was continuous with and redemptive of humanity at its best, its profoundest, its most spiritual, its sublimest. With this appeal uppermost in their minds, these nineteenth-century scholars worked at dogmatic and apologetic theology, at biblical exegesis, at homiletics and social ethics. As we have insisted above, much subsequent theology has been worked out in some relation or other to this type of thought; whether this relation has been that of sympathy or hostility, of continuity or discontinuity.

Much modern theology has taken the form of *dialogue* – of dialogue between Christian thought and secular science and philosophy, between the Church and the world, between the theologian and his intellectual contemporary who cannot share his religious convictions. Even that Church which has been traditionally considered, theologically speaking, the most conservative, the Roman Catholic Communion, has at last shown signs of being not unwilling to become a partner in the working out of such a mediating theology (see section 3 below). But a dialogue is a conversation between two sides. And of all styles perhaps dialogue is the most difficult to understand, because it involves us in grasping simultaneously two differing viewpoints which are trying to get in touch with each other. Our failure to grasp what one side or the other is trying to express must lead to failure in understanding the dialogue as a whole. This brief historical introduction is offered in the hope that it will assist the reader to enter sympathetically into some of those exciting dialogues which many are coming to regard as constituting the most promising growing-points of recent and contemporary theological thought.

FOR FURTHER READING

G. R. Cragg, *The Church and the Age of Reason, 1648–1789* (Pelican books, 1960).

John Macquarrie, *Twentieth-Century Religious Thought* (SCM Press, 1963).

John Macquarrie, *Contemporary Religious Thinkers* (SCM Press, 1968). (A companion volume of readings.)

B. M. G. Reardon, *Religious Thought in the Nineteenth Century* (Cambridge UP, 1966).

Alan Richardson (ed.), *A Dictionary of Christian Theology* (SCM Press, 1969).

James Richmond, *Faith and Philosophy* (Hodder and Stoughton, 1966).

A. R. Vidler, *The Church in an Age of Revolution* (Pelican books, 1961).

Heinz Zahrnt, *The Question of God* (Collins, 1969).

1

THEOLOGY OF THE WORD OF GOD

Karl Barth (1886-1968) was a Swiss Protestant theologian who has been one of the dominating figures of twentieth-century systematic theology. He received his theological education from leading liberal theologians, especially in the universities of Berlin and Marburg. Although initially an adherent of the ninteenth-century type of man-centred theology, he became, through reading the works of certain theological critics of Western Christendom such as Søren Kierkegaard (1813-55) and Feodor Dostoievsky (1821-81), and through disillusionment with that Western European culture which had tolerated and even helped to produce the explosive situation that led to the inhumanity of the First World War, violently opposed to the fundamental presuppositions, methods and aims of such theology. After the nineteen-twenties, Barth formulated his God-centred theology in his massive multi-volumed *Church Dogmatics*. Early in the nineteen-thirties Barth, while a theological professor at Bonn, helped to lead the theological opposition to the section of the German Church which was prepared to attempt a reconciliation between Christian teaching and the Nazi philosophy which claimed that the survival of Western civilization and culture depended upon the maintenance of racial distinctions and of the superiority (by force, if necessary) of the Germanic (or 'Aryan') racial group. Ejected from Germany by the State authorities, he became a professor in Basel in his native Switzerland, where he continued both his theological work and, until the end of the war, his opposition to the teachings and practices of Nazi Germany.

After he initiated his theological revolution (marked by the publication of his *Commentary on Romans* in 1918), Barth's fundamental presupposition was probably that Christian faith is absolutely unique, over against all other types of 'religion', in that it is engendered solely by the action and grace of God, who in his freedom and sovereignty is able to call into the situation of faith whomsoever he wills. Christian faith is produced solely by God's action upon man, never by man's attempt to think or to find God. Barth elaborated this basic principle of God as subject throughout all his writings with a rigid sternness, which he did not relent until almost the end of his life.

God is subject; as such it is he who stands over against man, revealing himself to man, speaking to man his Word of judgment and of grace, calling him, saving him, sending him. This, for Barth, is a description of the God of the Bible. All theological systems that suggest otherwise are uncompromisingly rejected. For example, theologies which allow that man can know something of God through rational speculation, through disciplined thought and reflection, are rejected as idolatrous. The God who is the *object* of such thought is a man-made idol, because the sovereign Lord of biblical revelation is always *subject*, never *object*. Almost the entire theological tradition of the nineteenth century is rejected; the nineteenth-century attempt to find God in human thought, feeling or moral striving was, according to Barth, disastrous, precisely because the attempt failed to distinguish between the 'God' who was the *object* of contemporary religiosity and speculation and 'God the Lord', who is utterly different from and apart from man, indescribably holy in comparison to sinful man, uttering that Word which not only saves but judges. Barth was always a stern critic of all *religion*: just because *religion* tries to construct God, to reach and possess him, it obstructs the sovereign Lord's free movement towards man in revelation and in grace. God moves towards man supremely in Jesus Christ, God's Word incarnate, as witnessed to by Holy Scripture. The heart and norm of Holy Scripture is simply and solely Jesus Christ, who is also the norm of the Church's preaching and life. Barth's theology is therefore sometimes correctly described as Christ-centred (christocentric).

His theology has evoked, since the nineteen-twenties, world-wide discussion, both in agreement and disagreement. His critics, both philosophers and theologians, have concentrated attention on his extremely negative attitude to human rationality and to man in his concrete actuality, as bearing God's image in himself as God's creature. One type of modern theology, the existentialist type (see section 2 below), has partly at least been a reaction against Barth's depreciation of man. And most theologians today would hesitate to identify themselves with Barth's polemic against speculative theology. Nevertheless, modern theology's enormous debt to Barth must not be overlooked. His theological enterprise has brought back into the centre of discussion the part that God's action plays in the birth of faith; that is, in the light of Barth's work, modern theologians are unable to discount theological categories such as revelation and grace. He has also brought sharply to the attention of religious thinkers once more the classical Christian stress on human fallenness, the notion that man, even at his very highest, is not God, and that all of man's thoughts, even at their sublimest, are not necessarily God's!

The relationship between the thought of Barth and that of other twentieth-century theologians is, if complex, very interesting. The later work of Dietrich Bonhoeffer, as evidenced in his *Letters and Papers from Prison* (see section 4 below), reveals his indebtedness to Barth, of whom he was an admirer. Bonhoeffer's rejection of *religion* (whether that of metaphysical speculation, of pious inwardness or of sectarian individualism) is of course extremely Barthian in tone and in motivation. Bonhoeffer's criticisms of Barth on the grounds that Barth, having correctly rejected *religion* as a prerequisite for Christian faith, wrongly retained *religious* terminology and jargon (terms such as justification, sanctification, propitiation and the like), thus failing to produce a 'non-religious interpretation of Christianity', is an interesting and important one. Strong tensions exist between Barth's thought and the work of theologians like Bultmann and Tillich (see section 2 below). While these latter two deplore Barth's doctrine of man as utterly depraved in his thinking and striving, Barth has vehemently insisted that Bultmann and Tillich, by trying to find a natural theology for the Gospel in man's despair, anxiety and conflicts, perpetuate what he considers to be the classical error of the nineteenth century, the failure to distinguish between God and man, and eventually make God in man's image. While Barth's work has been examined and expounded with sympathy and insight by Roman Catholic theologians (e.g. by Hans Urs von Balthasar and Hans Küng), he himself was critical of much Catholic theology. For instance, he suggested that the Roman Catholic Church has forgotten that God's Word in Jesus Christ is prior and superior both to the Church and to Scripture; that God's Word called into being both Church and Scripture; that the Church must be under the Word and not vice versa. He also criticized the defined position of the Roman Catholic magisterium as being in effect the imprisonment and manipulation of God's free and sovereign Word.

The not unknown temptation to dismiss Barth as a narrow, puritanical and irrational biblicist should be resisted. While he taught that man in his raw human nature does not and cannot know God by any of his innate powers, he also, paradoxically, devoted much energy to the attempt to evoke enthusiasm for the liberal theologian Schleiermacher and the composer Mozart. If he taught that God's image in man has been utterly defaced, from 1939 to 1945 he called upon the liberal democracies of the West to rise up and depose Hitler and his colleagues from a position of European supremacy. And in the late nineteen-fifties he was great enough to admit that many of the positions he adopted in the 'twenties, although historically justified, were too extreme (see his essay 'The Humanity of God'). Certainly, the debts owed him by systematic theology, by biblically based theology and by church life and preaching are incalculable.

FOR FURTHER READING

Karl Barth, *Dogmatics in Outline* (SCM Press 1949).
Against the Stream (SCM Press 1954).
From Rousseau to Ritschl (SCM Press, 1959).
The Humanity of God (Collins, 1961).

John Bowden, *Karl Barth* (SCM Press, 1971).

Karl Barth · *The Christian Understanding of Revelation*

I

Revelation means the publication of something private, something hidden. The Greek concept *Phanerosis* signifies the appearance of something hidden, and the parallel concept *Apokalypsis* the unveiling of something veiled. A closed door is opened; a covering removed. A light shines in the darkness, a question finds its answer, a puzzle its solution. In general terms, this is the process we call 'revelation'. In this general sense the concept covers many things that are not contained in the Christian connotation of revelation. Let us first make a brief survey of this general connotation of the term in ten points.

1. In the general sense of the term there are revelations which man may find good and useful, enriching and deepening his life, but which are not necessary, vital or indispensable. There are many things we do not need to know even if we could know them. Is there also such a thing as a necessary, and indispensable revelation?

2. There are revelations which man may find interesting, stimulating and exciting and possibly useful in some way or other, but which are nevertheless dangerous and therefore of doubtful value. As everyone knows, it has been questioned whether the revelation on the basis of which Prometheus discovered fire was not rather a curse for man, and the question is all the more pertinent in regard to the invention of gunpowder and certain discoveries which are making our own age so remarkable. Is there a revelation of which it can be said that it is clearly a good and wholesome revelation for man?

3. There are revelations which occur today and which may

be superseded by others tomorrow. There are therefore relative revelations. Is there, on the other hand, an absolute revelation, independent of the changes and chances of time?

4. There are revelations which are vouchsafed to possibly only a few, even very few people. There are therefore esoteric and exoteric relations to such revelations. Is there, in contrast to such special revelations, a general revelation which concerns all mankind?

5. There are revelations which are disclosures of matters of fact which were only temporarily unknown – that is, contingent revelations. Is there, in contrast to these, something like a necessary revelation?

6. There are revelations which consist in the translation into reality, life and activity of hidden but existing possibilities which are available to and can be realized by man. Is there, on the other hand, a revelation which cannot be effected by man at all, which does not consist in the realization of an existing possibility, but can only be interpreted as a gift?

7. There are revelations which, when they take place or have taken place, pass into human possession, so that man can muster them and do as he likes with them. Such revelations may be said to be open to exploitation. Is there, on the other hand, a free revelation, free in the sense that man cannot use it for his own purposes at all?

8. There are revelations which occur in the form of partial and approximate revelations in the course of intellectual inquiries, whether conducted by individuals or groups. Is there, in contrast to such merely approximate revelations, an original and definitive revelation?

9. There are revelations of which man can establish the existence, constitution and quality, and which he can contemplate with more or less pleasure and insight: we may call such revelations 'speculative' revelations. Is there, on the other hand, such a thing as a 'practical' revelation?

10. Everything that has been said so far may be summed up as the self-revelation of something that already exists, a self-revelation of man in the cosmos or a revelation of the cosmos

in relation to man: in other words, immanent, this-worldly revelation, which occurs in the human and cosmic realm. Is there, in contrast to this, such a thing as a transcendent, other-worldly revelation?

II

Revelation in the Christian sense is the wholly other revelation which only appears on the brink of all the above-mentioned possibilities.

Revelation in the Christian sense is:

1. A revelation which man needs not relatively, but absolutely, for his very life and being as man, a revelation without which he would not in fact be man at all, a revelation which decides being and non-being: in other words, one which man cannot please himself whether he accepts or not.

2. Revelation in the Christian sense is a revelation which accepts man absolutely, which takes place for his salvation, for his perfect salvation. Revelation in the Christian sense is an affirmation of man, however much it may be bound up with threats and judgments.

3. Revelation in the Christian sense is a revelation which was completely new to man yesterday and the day before yesterday, which is completely new to him today and will be new again tomorrow. It is absolute, not relative.

4. Revelation in the Christian sense is a revelation which comes to all men with equal strangeness from outside, but which concerns all men with equal intimacy. It is not a revelation intended for a few men only, but for all men.

5. Revelation in the Christian sense means the unveiling of certain facts that are fundamentally hidden from man, things no eye has seen, no ear has heard, no human heart conceived. Revelation in the Christian sense is not contingent.

6. Revelation in the Christian sense is the revelation of a reality outside man. It is the realization of a possibility which lies wholly in the place where the revelation takes place, not in the human realm. It is therefore a revelation which man is powerless to bring about by his own will.

7. Revelation in the Christian sense is a revelation which remains free in its relation to man. It cannot be capitalized.

8. Revelation in the Christian sense is a revelation which is complete and final, which fulfils past, present and future, which fulfils time itself. It is anything but merely approximate.

9. Revelation in the Christian sense is not an object which man can observe from outside; it is rather one which takes possession of man, seizes hold of him and calls him to action. It is anything but merely speculative.

10. We may sum up what has been said so far by saying that revelation in the Christian sense is the self-revelation of the Creator of all that is, the self-revelation of the Lord of all Being. It is not an immanent, this-worldy revelation, but comes from outside man and the cosmos. It is a transcendent revelation.

This is what is meant by revelation in the Christian sense of the term. It is useful to realize what revelation in this sense connotes, whatever the personal attitude may be that one adopts towards it. In any case it is the question we are to consider in this lecture.

We have seen that there are many kinds of revelation. In the ten points which we started with we tried to indicate the nature of the revelations that occur in all the spheres of human life, art, science, history, nature, and in man's personal life and experience. We contrasted this with the Christian understanding of revelation. You must decide for yourselves whether the two kinds are merely aspects of the same reality. But is it really feasible to lump together what we call revelation in all the fields of human experience and what the Christian means by the same term? Is it feasible, as happens so often, to derive, explain and justify the Christian interpretation on the basis of what we are in the habit of calling 'revelation' in everyday life? Is it even possible to compare the two realities? Is not revelation in the Christian sense rather a specific reality of its own, a revelation which begins at the very point where all the others end? We shall come back later to the significance, from the Christian point of view, of the existence of other revelations and meanings of revelation. What is certain is that Christian and non-Christian revelations are two quite distinct realities which must not be confused. We are concerned here with the sphere of Christian revelation which cannot be seen or penetrated from the sphere of any other revelation, but which has a special content and constitutes a special order of its own.

Revelation in the Christian sense is the revelation of God. For the Christian there is no need of a special enquiry and a special proof to know and to declare who and what God is. For the Christian the revelation is itself the proof, the proof furnished by God himself. The Christian answer to the question as to who and what God is, is a simple one: he is the subject who acts in his revelation. This act of revelation is a token of his Being and the expression of his nature.

III

Keeping to the sequence of our original ten points, we may define the Christian understanding of God as follows:

Who is God?

1. God is he who is absolutely necessary to man. God decides man's being or non-being.

2. God is he who accepts man with the utmost seriousness and in the deepest love. He is his saviour.

3. God is he who was, who is and always will be new to man. He is absolute.

4. God is he who is above all and for all: 'Before thee none can boast but all must fear.'

5. God is he who meets man as the inherently necessary and fundamentally hidden reality.

6. God is he who is able to come quite close to man, though he is the farthest away from him. Though unknown, he is able to become most intimately known to man.

7. God is he who in revealing himself to man, is and remains free.

8. God is he who was, is and shall be, the Lord of time, the eternal God, the God of the aeons.

9. God is also the Lord and Master of man, who makes demands on man.

10. God is the Creator and as such acts upon man, without whom no other being, including man, could exist.

God is he who acts in his revelation and thereby describes himself. The revelation of God, that is, the action of the Subject who reveals himself in this revelation, is what is meant when Christians speak of revelation. They mean the revelation of this God, the one, the only God. There seem to be many gods, just as there are many revelations. In accordance with this multiplicity of revelations there are many religions, theologies, philosophies, ideologies and, therefore, many and multiform images of God. Sometimes God is said to be that which is most necessary or even most dangerous to man, sometimes he is merely a general ideal or an individual dream, sometimes the embodiment of an historical ideal or a temporary exigency, sometimes the essence of the universal cosmic possibilities of man in their known and unknown depths. Sometimes God may be the longed-for opium of a personal or general development, sometimes the exponent of some human caprice; ultimately and really all these gods are simply some form of man himself in his relationship to the cosmos. I must leave you to decide for yourselves whether God, in the Christian understanding of revelation, is simply one of these gods, or whether the *Deus non est in genere* (Tertullian) is not true, whether the antithesis between the true God and the false gods, the 'nonentities', as the Old Testament calls them, is not valid and true. God is not an abstract category by which even the Christian understanding of the word has to be measured, but he who is called God here is the One God, the Single God, the Sole God.

IV

What is this revelation, what is the subject of the revelation of which we have been speaking? What is the frame of mind which is open to receive what we call revelation? What is the theory of cognition for which revelation in the Christian sense is a valid object of knowledge?

And on the other hand: is there a conception of the world, a basic view of existence which can include what we have called God? If the general conception of the world and the general pattern of human thought are the criteria, can such a thing as revelation in the Christian sense exist at all? Does this God exist, of whom we have spoken as the subject of this revelation? What are we in fact talking about? Are we possibly talking nonsense, talking about *non-ens*? There are theories of knowledge which can account for what we have called the self-revelation of that which exists, and there are ontologies which can embrace the gods corresponding to these revelations. But as far as one can see there is no theory of knowledge and no pattern of thought which can embrace revelation in the Christian sense of the term. We can work through the whole history of philosophy from Thales to Martin Heidegger, and we shall be forced to the same conclusion. There is no room for revelation in the Christian sense in any human inquiry or any human faculty of reason. And the same applies to what we have called God in the Christian sense. There may be conceptions of the world which provide for gods, but the God of Christianity cannot appear in any imaginable human conception of the world. Try to map out a conception of the world in which God, as understood in Christian thought, would have room! And so we must say that if a purely human conception of the world is the measure of all things, then neither revelation nor God in the Christian sense exist at all. We would in fact have been speaking about 'nothing' when we were speaking about revelation and God.

We have not, however, been speaking about 'nothing', but about a reality, something incomparably more real than anything that can be called real in the sphere of human thought and knowledge. When the Christian language speaks of revelation and God it means a reality which is very insignificant-looking and outwardly most unpromising; it speaks quite simply of a single concrete fact in the midst of the numberless host of facts and the vast stream of historical events; it speaks of a single human person living in the age of the Roman Empire: it speaks of Jesus Christ. When the Christian language speaks of God it does so not on the basis of some speculation or other, but looking at this fact, this story, this person. It cannot place this fact in relationship to any system of principles and ideas which would illuminate its importance and significance; it cannot explain and establish it from any other source; it makes no presuppositions when it points to this event. Its sole concern is with the event itself; all it can do is to refer to the existence, or rather, more precisely, the presence of this fact and the reception of the news of its presence as recorded in a tiny sheaf of news about the existence of this Person.

With its eyes concentrated on this news, Christianity speaks of revelation and of God as the subject of this revelation. Looking at this fact, it speaks with absolute assurance. Here – but only here – it sees revelation (in the sense of the criteria we have stated) and it sees God (again, in the sense of the criteria we have stated). Revelation in the Christian sense takes place and God in the Christian sense is, in accordance with the news of Jesus Christ, his words and deeds, his death and resurrection. . . .

Inasmuch as this creative Word, which is superior to all being, is spoken and heard in him, revelation takes place: transcendent, not immanent revelation. Revelation from the origin of all being. And it is God who speaks this Word.

The concept of revelation and the concept of God in the Christian sense coincide, therefore, in the contemplation of Jesus Christ, in which they are both related to reality. And in contemplation of him it is decided that God is and what God is; that God is a person and not a neutral thing. And that revelation is his acting and speaking and not a blind occurrence or an unarticulated sound.

2

EXISTENTIALISM AND BEYOND

PROBABLY the best-known theologian who has tried to present the Christian message in the language and concepts of existentialist thought is **Rudolf Bultmann** (1884-), who was Professor of New Testament at the University of Marburg from 1921 until 1951. Since the nineteen-twenties, Bultmann has approached his theological work in the light of the understanding of man's life that we find in the writings of the existentialist thinker Martin Heidegger (1889-). While Bultmann has an affinity with Barth in holding that in the last analysis man's knowledge of and relationship to God is dependent upon the Christian message which is addressed to him as a sinner in need of grace, he differs from Barth in two related ways. First, he holds that there is a sense in which man's coming to believe depends upon how man understands his own existence. That is, God's Word can only really strike home to the man who is, as a concrete historical agent, struggling with profound problems concerning his life, its problems and its aim. And second, he makes much more than does Barth of the conceptual and terminological difficulties in which modern man is involved when he reads the Bible or when the Christian gospel is proclaimed to him. According to Bultmann, so much has happened to human thinking and talking since the time when the New Testament was written that it is today almost incomprehensible to man. Bultmann has indicated this unintelligibility by using the term *myth.* Biblical language is *mythological* in that it expresses a way of looking at the world, a way of thinking about God, a cosmology, and understanding of nature, which are radically different from those of the contemporary world.

According to Bultmann, the task facing the theologian (and,

it must be stressed, the pastor and teacher) is to transpose this mythological language into discourse which will strike forcibly home to contemporary man, showing him that what the Bible is talking about has something to do *with him*, to do with a way of life which is a new and redemptive possibility *for him*. But in order to find a new and relevant speech, Bultmann has utilized the work of the philosopher Heidegger. Heidegger is an *existentialist* – that is, he holds that *human existence* is absolutely unique in reality. Human beings exist in a way in which nothing else can be said to exist. To understand humans in the same way in which we grasp natural things, events and objects is gravely erroneous. Heidegger can therefore be described as an anti-positivist (see Historical Introduction above). He emphatically rejects the view that *all* of our knowledge is acquired by scientific procedures; on the contrary, the most significant knowledge we can acquire, knowledge of our own personal being, can be gained only by ourselves in actually living our lives. Heidegger gives a picture of man in a twofold way: first, he shows how man can live an anonymous life as a mere part of the lump of humanity, depersonalized, being moulded by the forces which press in upon him from his environment, swept purposelessly along like a mere branch in the stream of life, never becoming anything in particular; second, he shows how man can live a meaningful life by taking with utter seriousness the possibilities which are uniquely his, by attempting through decision to modify what he has become through his false, depersonalized past, so that his life becomes oriented towards the future where his real, authentic self may be achieved. In this way, man ceases to be merely an item of nature and becomes also a free agent living in the dimension of history.

Bultmann has utilized at least the formal structure of Heidegger's thought in reformulating the Christian message for modern times. He has attempted to show that in the human situation portrayed by Heidegger the Christian message can come to possess tremendous relevance, if it is *demythologized*. That is, if its mythological language is translated completely into existential language; i.e., language referring to human existence, its conflicts and possibilities. But, of course, in making these proposals, Bultmann has evoked considerable criticism, and indeed, has initiated a world-wide controversy which has tended to dominate the theological world since just before 1950. In particular, critics have asked if by confining Christianity exclusively to the existential sphere Bultmann's theology can possibly do justice to certain indispensable aspects of Christian thought. For example, by heavily stressing the contemporary existential relevance of the Gospel does not Bultmann thereby overlook the *past-historical* dimension in Christianity? Or, by refusing to speak of God in other than existential terms, does not he thereby give a reduced and shrunken conception of God, in that he cannot say anything about God apart from God in relation to man? What about God as he is in his essence? Can we not say something of God as he is in himself, apart from God and the world? Questions such as these have been asked in the controversy. Apart from the specific answers we give to these questions, it can hardly be denied that Bultmann has made Christian theology a talking-point in the post-war world and has made the Christian understanding of life a highly relevant possibility for contemporary man, especially in so far as he is alarmed by the dehumanization implicit in modern technological mass-societies.

The article by Bultmann which sparked off the 'demythologization' debate is printed (with reactions) in H. W. Bartsch (ed.), *Kerygma and Myth* (SPCK), 1953). Essays outlining the basic ideas of his theology are collected in Rudolf Bultmann, *Faith and Understanding* (SCM Press, 1969); the best detailed introduction to his thought is W. Schmithals, *An Introduction to the Theology of Rudolf Bultmann* (SCM Press, 1968).

Rudolf Bultmann · *Jesus Christ and Mythology*

The whole conception of the world which is presupposed in the preaching of Jesus as in the New Testament generally is mythological; i.e., the conception of the world as being structured in three storeys, heaven, earth and hell; the conception of the intervention of supernatural powers in the cause of events; and the conception of miracles, especially the conception of the intervention of supernatural powers in the inner life of the soul, the conception that men can be tempted and corrupted by the devil and possessed by evil spirits. This conception of the world we call mythological because it is different from the conception of the world which has been formed and developed by science since its inception in ancient Greece and which has been accepted by all modern men. In this modern conception of the world the cause-and-effect nexus is fundamental. Though modern physical theories take account of chance in the chain of cause and effect in subatomic phenomena, our daily living, purposes and actions are not affected. In any case, modern science does not believe that the course of nature can be interpreted, or, so to speak, perforated, by supernatural powers.

The same is true of the modern study of history, which does not take into account any intervention of God or of the devil or of demons in the course of history. Instead, the course of history is considered to be an unbroken whole, complete in itself, though differing from the course of nature because there are in history spiritual powers which influence the will of persons. Granted that not all historical events are determined by physical necessity and that persons are responsible for their actions, nevertheless nothing happens without rational motivation. Otherwise, responsibility would be dissolved. Of course, there are still many superstitions among modern men, but they are exceptions or even anomalies. Modern men take it for granted that the course of nature and of history, like their own inner life and their practical life, is nowhere interrupted by the intervention of supernatural powers.

Then the question inevitably arises: is it possible that Jesus' preaching of the Kingdom of God still has any importance for modern men and the preaching of the New Testament as a whole is still important for modern men? The preaching of the New Testament proclaims Jesus Christ, not only his preaching of the Kingdom of God but first of all his person, which was mythologized from the very beginnings of earliest Christianity. New Testament scholars are at variance as to whether Jesus himself claimed to be the Messiah, the King of the time of blessedness, whether he believed himself to be the Son of Man who would come on the clouds of heaven. If so, Jesus understood himself in the light of mythology. We need not, at this point, decide one way or the other. At any rate, the early Christian community thus regarded him as a mythological figure. It expected him to return as the Son of Man on the clouds of heaven to bring salvation and damnation as judge of the world. His person is viewed in the light of mythology when he is said to have been begotten of the Holy Spirit and born of a virgin, and this becomes clearer still in Hellenistic Christian communities where he is understood to be the Son of God in a metaphysical sense, a great, pre-existent heavenly being who became man for the sake of our redemption and took on himself suffering, even the suffering of the cross. It is evident that such conceptions are mythological, for they were widespread in the mythologies of Jews and Gentiles and then were transferred to the historical person of Jesus. Particularly the conception of the pre-existent Son of God who descended in human guise into the world to redeem mankind is part of the Gnostic doctrine of redemption, and nobody hesitates to call this doctrine mythological. This raises in an acute form the question: *what is the importance of the preaching of Jesus and of the preaching of the New Testament as a whole for modern man?*

For modern man the mythological conception of the world, the conceptions of eschatology, of redeemer and of redemption, are over and done with. Is it possible to expect that we shall make a sacrifice of understanding, *sacrificium intellectus*, in order to accept what we cannot sincerely consider true – namely because such conceptions are suggested by the Bible? Or ought we to pass over those sayings of the New Testament which contain such mythological conceptions and to select other sayings which are not such stumbling-blocks to modern man? In fact, the preaching of Jesus is not confined to eschatological sayings.

He proclaimed also the will of God, which is God's demand, the demand for the good. Jesus demands truthfulness and purity, readiness to sacrifice and to love. He demands that the whole man be obedient to God, and he protests against the delusion that one's duty to God can be fulfilled by obeying certain external commandments. If the ethical demands of Jesus are stumbling-blocks to modern man, then it is to his selfish will, not to his understanding, that they are stumbling-blocks.

What follows from all this? Shall we retain the ethical preaching of Jesus and abandon his eschatological preaching? Shall we reduce his preaching of the Kingdom of God to the so-called social gospel? Or is there a third possibility? We must ask whether the eschatological preaching and the mythological sayings as a whole contain a still deeper meaning which is concealed under the cover of mythology. If that is so, let us abandon the mythological conceptions precisely because we want to retain their deeper meaning. This method of interpretation of the New Testament which tries to recover the deeper meaning behind the mythological conceptions I call *de-mythologizing* – an unsatisfactory word, to be sure. Its aim is not to eliminate the mythological statements but to interpret them.

An objection often heard against the attempt to de-mythologize is that it takes the modern world-view as the criterion of the interpretation of the Scripture and the Christian message and that Scripture and Christian message are not allowed to say anything that is in contradiction with the modern world-view.

It is, of course, true that de-mythologizing takes the modern world-view as a criterion. To de-mythologize is to reject not Scripture or the Christian message as a whole, but the world-view of Scripture, which is the world-view of a past epoch, which all too often is retained in Christian dogmatics and in the preaching of the Church. To de-mythologize is to deny that the message of Scripture and of the Church is bound to an ancient world-view which is obsolete.

The attempt to de-mythologize begins with this important insight: Christian preaching, in so far as it is preaching of the

Word of God by God's command and in his name, does not offer a doctrine which can be accepted either by reason or by a *sacrificium intellectus*. Christian preaching is *kerygma*, that is, a proclamation addressed not to the theoretical reason, but to the hearer as a self. In this manner Paul commends himself to every man's conscience in the sight of God (II Cor. 4.2). De-mythologizing will make clear this function of preaching as a personal message, and in doing so it will eliminate a false stumbling-block and bring into sharp focus the real stumbling-block, the word of the cross.

Thus it follows that the objection is raised by a mistake, namely, the objection that de-mythologizing dissolves the message into a product of human rational thinking, and that the mystery of God is destroyed by de-mythologizing. Not at all! On the contrary, de-mythologizing makes clear the true meaning of God's mystery. The incomprehensibility of God lies not in the sphere of theoretical thought but in the sphere of personal existence.

Over and over again I hear the objection that de-mythologizing transforms Christian faith into philosophy. This objection arises from the fact that I call de-mythologizing an interpretation, an existentialist interpretation, and that I make use of conceptions developed especially by Martin Heidegger in existentialist philosophy.

We can understand the problem best when we remember that *de-mythologizing is an hermeneutic method*, that is, a method of interpretation, of exegesis. 'Hermeneutics' means the art of exegesis.

Reflection on hermeneutics (the method of interpretation) makes it clear that interpretation, that is, exegesis, is always based on principles and conceptions which guide exegesis as presuppositions, although interpreters are often not aware of this fact.

Every interpreter brings with him certain conceptions, perhaps idealistic or psychological, as presuppositions of his exegesis, in most cases unconsciously. But then the question arises, which conceptions are right and adequate? Which presuppositions are right and adequate? Or is it perhaps impossible to give an answer to these questions?

Should we perhaps say that we must interpret without any presupposition; that the text itself provides the conceptions of exegesis? This is sometimes asserted, but it is impossible. To be sure, our exegesis must be without presuppositions with regard to the results of our exegesis. We cannot know in advance what the text will say; on the contrary, we must learn from it. An exegesis which, for example, makes the presupposition that its results must agree with some dogmatic statement is not a real and fair exegesis. There is, however, a difference in principle between presuppositions in respect of results and presuppositions in respect of method. It can be said that method is nothing other than a kind of questioning, a way of putting questions. This means that I cannot understand a given text without asking certain questions of it. The questions may differ very widely. If you are interested in psychology, you will read the Bible – or any other literature – asking questions about psychological phenomena.

You can read and interpret a text with other interests, for example, with aesthetical or with historical interest, with the interest in political or cultural history of states, etc. The basic presupposition for every form of exegesis is that your own relation to the subject-matter prompts the question you bring to the text and elicits the answers you obtain from the text.

Now, when we interpret the Bible, what is our interest? Certainly the Bible is an historical document and we must interpret the Bible by the methods of historical research. We must study the language of the Bible, the historical situation of the biblical authors, etc. But what is our true and real interest? Are we to read the Bible only as an historical document in order to reconstruct an epoch of past history for which the Bible serves as a 'source'? Or is it more than a source? I think our interest is really to hear what the Bible has to say for our actual present, to hear what is the truth about our life and about our soul.

Now the question arises as to which is the adequate method, which are the adequate conceptions? And also, which is the relation, the 'life-relation', which we have in advance, to the theme of the Bible from which our questions and our conceptions arise? Must we say that we do not have such relation in advance, since the theme of the Bible is the only revelation of God, and we can gain a relation to God only by his revelation and not in advance of it?

Indeed, there are theologians who have argued in this manner, but it seems to me that they are in error. Man does have in advance a relation to God which has found its classical expression in the words of Augustine: 'Thou hast made us for thyself, and our heart is restless, until it rests in thee.' Man has a knowledge of God in advance, though not of the revelation of God, that is, of his action in Christ. He has a relation to God in his search for God, conscious or unconscious. Man's life is moved by the search for God because it is always moved, consciously or unconsciously, by the question about his own personal existence. The question of God and the question of myself are identical.

Now we have found the adequate way to put the question when we interpret the Bible. This question is, *how is man's existence understood in the Bible?* I approach the biblical texts with this question for the same reason which supplies the deepest motive for all historical research and for all interpretation of historical documents.

The interpretation of the biblical scriptures, however, has a special motive. The tradition and the preaching of the Church tells us that we are to hear in the Bible authoritative words about our existence. What distinguishes the Bible from other literature is that in the Bible a certain possibility of existence is shown to me not as something which I am free to choose or to refuse. Rather, the Bible becomes for me a word addressed personally to me, which not only informs me about existence in general, but gives me real existence. This, however, is a possibility on which I cannot count in advance. It is not a methodological presupposition by means of which I can understand the Bible. For this possibility can become a reality only when I understand the word.

Our task, therefore, is to discover the hermeneutical principle by which we can understand what is said in the Bible. If it is true that the right questions are concerned with the possibilities of understanding human existence, then it is necessary to discover the adequate conceptions by which such understanding is to be expressed. To discover these conceptions is the task of philosophy.

But now the objection is brought forward that exegesis falls under the control of philosophy. This is the case indeed, but we must ask in what sense it is so. It is an illusion to hold that any exegesis can be independent of secular conceptions. Every interpreter is inescapably dependent on conceptions which he has inherited from a tradition, consciously or unconsciously, and every tradition is dependent on some philosophy or other.

At this point we must realize that there will never be a right philosophy in the sense of an absolutely perfect system, a philosophy which could give answers to all questions and clear up all riddles of human existence. Our question is simply which philosophy today offers the most adequate perspective and conceptions for understanding human existence. Here it seems to me that we should learn from existentialist philosophy, because in this philosophical school human existence is directly the object of attention. Existentialist philosophy, while it gives no answer to the question of my personal existence, makes personal existence my own personal responsibility, and by doing so it helps to make me open to the word of the Bible.

It is often said that it is impossible to carry through demythologizing consistently, since, if the message of the New Testament is to be retained at all, we are bound to speak of God as acting. In such speech there remains a mythological residue. For is it not mythological to speak of God as acting?

How must we speak of God as acting if our speech is not to be understood as mythological speech? God as acting does not refer to an event which can be perceived by me without myself being drawn into the event as into God's action, without myself taking part in it as being acted upon. In other words, to speak of God as acting involves the events of personal existence. The encounter with God can be an event for man only here and now, since man lives within the limits of space and time. When we speak of God as acting, we mean that we are confronted with God, addressed, asked, judged, or blessed by God. Therefore, to speak in this manner is not to speak in symbols or images, but to speak analogically. For when we speak in this manner of God as acting, we conceive God's action as an analogue to the actions taking place between men. Moreover, we conceive the communion between God and man as an analogue to the communion between man and man. It is in this analogical sense that we speak of God's love and care for men, of his demands and of his wrath, of his promise and grace, and it is in this analogical sense that we call him Father.

At this point a really important objection arises. If what we have said is correct, does it not follow that God's action is deprived of objective reality, that it is reduced to a purely subjective, psychological experience (*Erlebnis*); that God exists only as an inner event in the soul, whereas faith has real meaning only if God exists outside the believer? Such objections are brought forward again and again, and the shades of Schleiermacher and Feuerbach are conjured up in this controversy. *Erlebnis* (psychological experience) was indeed a popular catchword in German theology before the First World War. Faith was often described as *Erlebnis*. It was on this catchword that Karl Barth and the so-called dialectical theologians made an all-out attack.

When we say that to speak of God means to speak of our own personal existence, the meaning is a totally different one. The objection which I have just summarized suffers from a psychological misunderstanding of the life of the soul. From the statement that to speak of God is to speak of myself, it by no means follows that God is not outside the believer. (This would be the case only if faith is interpreted as a purely psychological event.)

When man is understood in the genuine sense as an historical being which has its reality in concrete situations and decisions, in the very encounters of life, it is clear, on the one hand, that faith, speaking of God as acting, cannot defend itself against the charge of being an illusion, and, on the other hand, that faith does not mean a psychologically subjective event.

Is it enough to say that faith grows out of the encounter with the Holy Scriptures as the Word of God, that faith is nothing but simple hearing? The answer is yes. But this answer is valid only if the Scriptures are understood neither as a manual of doctrine nor as a record of witnesses to a faith which I interpret by sympathy and empathy. On the contrary, to hear the Scriptures as the Word of God means to hear them as a word which is addressed to me, as *kerygma*, as a proclamation. Then my understanding is not a neutral one, but rather my response to a call. The fact that the word of the Scriptures is God's Word cannot be demonstrated objectively; it is an event which happens here and now. God's Word is hidden in the Scriptures as each action of God is hidden everywhere.

Paul Tillich (1886-1965) was a German Protestant philosophical theologian who, after holding academic posts in Marburg, Dresden and Frankfurt, was forced to leave Nazi Germany in 1933 because of his political views. He held several chairs of theology in the United States from 1933 until his death in 1965. His thought became increasingly influential in America, especially through his three-volume *Systematic Theology* (Nisbet).

Like Bultmann, Tillich believed that theology must begin with the human situation; theologians must immerse themselves in the societies in which they live, and must share with secular man the sufferings, ambiguities and conflicts to which he is subject; using the insights of existentialist thought, psychoanalysis and the arts, they must make an analysis of the human situation in the form of profound questions; their theological raw materials, given in Scripture, tradition and Christian experience, are *correlated* with these questions. Theological method for Tillich was therefore a business of fitting together question and answer, it was a *method of correlation*. But, Tillich insisted, the questions actually asked by men have their ultimate source in God, who as Creator is responsible for the essential structure of human existence. Tillich differed from Bultmann in certain significant aspects. For one thing, he was much more 'intellectualistic' than Bultmann, in that he held that man's *philosophical* quest, in which man raised questions about the nature and meaning of being, led to God, who is Being-Itself or the Ground of Being. For another, Tillich had a different and probably higher conception of myths and symbols than has Bultmann. Tillich was a fine preacher, as well as a profound theologian, and his sermons, *The Shaking of the Foundations* (Penguin), *The New Being* and *The Eternal Now* (Fontana) are as good an introduction to his thought as any. *Perspectives on 19th and 20th Century Protestant Theology* (SCM Press, 1967) relates Tillich to his historical background, and *My Travel Diary*: *1936* (SCM Press, 1970) is a first-hand portrait of the man.

Paul Tillich · *The Divine Name*

'*You shall not take the name of the Lord your God in vain: for the Lord will not hold him guiltless who takes his name in vain.*' Exodus 20.7.

There must be something extraordinary about the name if the second commandment tries to protect it as the other commandments try to protect life, honour, property. Of course, God need not protect himself, but he does protect his name, and so seriously that he adds to this single commandment a special threat. This is done because, within the name, that which bears the name is present. In ancient times, one believed that one held in one's power the being whose hidden name one knew. One believed that the saviour-god conquered the demons by discovering the mystery of the power embodied in their names, just as we today try to find out the hidden names of the powers that disrupt our unconscious depths and drive us to mental disturbances. If we gain insight into their hidden striving, we break their power. Men have always tried to use the divine name in the same way, not in order to break its power, but to harness its power for their own uses. Calling on the name of God in prayer, for instance, can mean attempting to make God a tool for our purposes. A name is never an empty sound; it is a bearer of power; it gives Spiritual Presence to the unseen. This is the reason the divine name can be taken in vain, and why one may destroy oneself by taking it in vain. For the invocation of the holy does not leave us unaffected. If it does not heal us, it may disintegrate us. This is the seriousness of the use of the divine name. This is the danger of religion, and even of anti-religion. For in both the name of God is used as well as misused.

Let me speak to you today of the danger of the use of the word God, when it is both denied and affirmed, and of the sublime embarrassment that we feel when we say 'God'. We may distinguish three forms of such embarrassment: the embarrassment of tact, the embarrassment of doubt, and the embarrassment of awe.

I

Not long ago, an intellectual leader was reported as saying, 'I hope for the day when everyone can speak again of God without embarrassment.' These words, seriously meant, deserve thoughtful consideration, especially in view of the fact that the last fifteen years have brought to this country an immense increase in the willingness to use the name of God – an unquestionable and astonishing revival, if not of religion, certainly of religious awareness. Do we hope that this will lead us to a state in which the name of God will be used without sublime embarrassment, without the restriction imposed by the fact that in the divine name there is more present than the name? Is an unembarrassed use of the divine name desirable? Is unembarrassed religion desirable? Certainly not! For the Presence of the Divine in the name demands a shy and trembling heart.

Everyone at one time or another finds himself in a situation where he must decide whether he shall use or avoid the name of God, whether he shall talk with personal involvement about religious matters, either for or against them. Making such a decision is often difficult. We feel that we should remain silent in certain groups of people because it might be tactless to introduce the name of God, or even to talk about religion. But our attitude is not unambiguous. We believe we are being tactful, when actually we may be cowardly. And then sometimes we accuse ourselves of cowardice, although it is really tact that prevents us from speaking out. This happens not only to those who would speak out *for* God, but also to those who would speak out *against* God. Whether for or against him, his name is on our lips and we are embarrassed because we feel that more is at stake than social tact. So we keep silent, uncertain as to whether we are right or wrong. The situation itself is uncertain.

Perhaps we might isolate ourselves or seem ridiculous by even mentioning the divine name, affirming or denying it. But there might also be another present for whom the mention of the divine name would produce a first experience of the Spiritual Presence and a decisive moment in his life. And again, perhaps there may be someone for whom a tactless allusion to God would evoke a definite sense of repulsion against religion. He may now think that religion *as such* is an abuse of the name of God. No one can look into the hearts of others, even if he converses with them intimately. We must risk *now* to talk courageously and *now* to keep silent tactfully. But in no case should we be pushed into a direct affirmation or denial of God which lacks the tact that is born of awe. The sublime embarrassment about his real presence in and through his name should never leave us.

Many persons have felt the pain of this embarrassment when they have had to teach their children the divine name, and others have felt it perhaps when they tried to protect their children against a divine name that they considered an expression of dangerous superstition. It seems natural to teach children about most objects in nature and history without embarrassment, and there are parents who think it is equally natural to teach them divine things. But I believe that many of us as parents in this situation feel a sublime embarrassment. We know as Jesus knew that children are more open to the divine Presence than adults. It may well be, however, that if we use the divine name easily, we may close this openness and leave our children insensitive to the depth and the mystery of what is present in the divine name. But if we try to withhold it from them, whether because we affirm or because we deny it, emptiness may take hold of their hearts, and they may accuse us later of having cut them off from the most important thing in life. A Spirit-inspired tact is necessary in order to find the right way between these dangers. No technical skill or psychological knowledge can replace the sublimely embarrassed mind of parents or teachers, and especially of teachers of religion.

There is a form of misuse of the name of God that offends those who hear it with a sensitive ear, just because it did not worry those who misused it without sensitivity. I speak now of a public use of the name of God which has little to do with God, but much to do with human purpose – good or bad. Those of us who are grasped by the mystery present in the name of God are often stung when this name is used in governmental and political speeches, in opening prayers for conferences and dinners, in secular and religious advertisements, and in international war propaganda. Often the frequent use of the name of God is praised, as this is an indication that we are a religious nation. And one boasts of this, comparing one's nation with others. Should this be condemned? It is hard *not* to do so, but neither is it easy. If the divine name is used publicly with full conviction, and therefore with embarrassment and spiritual tact, it may be used without offence, although this is hardly ever so. It is usually taken in vain when used for purposes that are not to the glory of his name.

II

There is another more basic cause for sublime embarrassment about using the divine name – the doubt about God himself.

Such doubt is universally human, and God would not be God if we could possess him like any object of our familiar world, and verify his reality like any other reality under inquiry. Unless doubt is conquered, there is no faith. Faith must overcome something; it must leap over the ordinary processes that provide evidence, because its object lies above the whole realm where scientific verification is possible. Faith is the courage that conquers doubt, not by removing it, but by taking it as an element into itself. I am convinced that the element of doubt, conquered in faith, is never completely lacking in any serious affirmation of God. It is not always on the surface; but it always gnaws at the depth of our being. We may know people intimately who have a seemingly primitive unshaken faith, but it is not difficult to discover the underswell of doubt that in critical moments surges up to the surface. Religious leaders tell us both directly and indirectly of the struggle in their minds between faith and unfaith. From fanatics of faith we hear beneath their unquestioning affirmations of God the shrill sound of their repressed doubt. It is repressed, but not annihilated.

On the other hand, listening to the cynical denials of God that are an expression of the flight from a meaning of life, we hear the voice of a carefully covered despair, a despair that demonstrates not assurance but doubt about their negation. And in our encounter with those who assume scientific reasons to deny God, we find that they are certain of their denial only so long as they battle – and rightly so – against superstitious ideas of God. When, however, they ask the question of God who is really God – namely, the question of the meaning of life as a whole and their own life, including their scientific work, their self-assurance tumbles, for neither he who affirms nor he who denies God can be ultimately certain about his affirmation or his denial.

Doubt, and not certitude, is our human situation, whether we affirm or deny God. And perhaps the difference between them is not so great as one usually thinks. They are probably very similar in their mixture of faith and doubt. Therefore, the denial of God, if serious, should not shake us. What should trouble everyone who takes life seriously is the existence of indifference. For he who is indifferent, when hearing the name of God, and feels, at the same time, that the meaning of his life is being questioned, denies his true humanity.

It is doubt in the depth of faith that often produces sublime embarrassment. Such embarrassment can be an expression of conscious or unconscious honesty. Have we not felt how something in us sometimes makes us stop, perhaps only for one moment, when we want to say 'God'? This moment of hesitation may express a deep feeling for God. It says something about the power of the divine name, and it says something about him who hesitates to use it. Sometimes we hesitate to use the word 'God' even without words, when we are alone; we may hesitate to speak to God even privately and voicelessly, as in prayer. It may be that doubt prevents us from praying. And beyond this we may feel that the abyss between God and us makes the use of his name impossible for us; we do not dare to speak to him, because we feel him standing on the other side of the abyss from us. This can be a profound affirmation of him. The silent embarrassment of using the divine name can protect us against violating the divine mystery.

III

We have considered the silence of tact and the silence of honesty concerning the divine name. But behind them both lies something more fundamental, the silence of awe, that seems to prohibit the speaking of God altogether. But is this the last word demanded by the divine mystery? Must we spread silence around what concerns us more than anything else – the meaning of our existence? The answer is – no! For God himself has given mankind names for himself in those moments when he has broken into our finitude and made himself manifest. We can and must use these names. For silence has power only if it is the other side of speaking, and in this way becomes itself a kind of speaking. This necessity is both our justification and our being judged, when we gather together in the name of God. We are an assembly where we speak about God. We are a church. The church is the place where the mystery of the holy should be experienced with awe and sacred embarrassment. But is this our experience? Are our prayers, communal or personal, a use or a misuse of the divine name? Do we feel the sublime embarrassment that so many people outside the churches feel? Are we gripped by awe when, as ministers, we point to the Divine Presence in the sacraments? Or, as theological interpreters of the holy, are we too sure that we can really explain him to others? Is there enough sacred embarrassment in us when fluent biblical quotations or quick, mechanized words of prayer pour from our mouths? Do we preserve the respectful distance from the Holy-Itself, when we claim to have the truth about him, or to be at the place of his Presence or to be the administrators of his Power – the proprietors of the Christ? How much embarrassment, how much awe is alive in Sunday devotional services all over the world?

And now let me ask the Church and all its members, including you and myself, a bold question. Could it be that, in order to judge the misuse of his name within the Church, God reveals himself from time to time by creating silence about himself? Could it be that sometimes he prevents the use of his name in order to protect his name, that he withholds from a generation what was natural to previous generations – the use of the word God? Could it be that godlessness is not caused only by human resistance, but also by God's paradoxical action – using men and the forces by which they are driven to judge the assemblies that gather in his name and take his name in vain? Is the secular silence about God that we experience everywhere today perhaps God's way of forcing his Church back to a sacred embarrassment when speaking of him? It may be bold to ask such questions. Certainly there can be no answer, because we do not know the character of the divine providence. But even without an answer, the question itself should warn all those inside the Church to whom the use of his name comes too easily.

Let me close with a few words that are both personal and more than personal. While thinking about this sermon I tried to make it not only one about the divine name, but also about God himself. Such an attempt stands under the judgment of the very commandment I tried to interpret, for it was a refined way of taking the name of God in vain. We can speak only of the names through which he has made himself known to us. For he himself 'lives in unapproachable light, whom no man has ever seen nor can see'.

Martin Buber (1878-1965) was a Jewish philosopher and theologian who worked in Germany until 1938; from 1938 until 1951 he was Professor of Social Philosophy at the Hebrew University in Jerusalem. His work (especially his epoch-making *I and Thou* (T. and T. Clark, 1937)) has been profoundly influential not only in philosophy and theology but also in education, psychiatry, sociology and aesthetics. Buber carefully distinguished between two fundamental human attitudes which he labelled *I-It* and *I-Thou.* While both of these are indispensable to man's life in the world, Buber believed that it was in the second that man's truly authentic personal being is brought to maturity. He developed the view that the *I-Thou* life of dialogue, of mutuality, led towards God, the eternal *Thou.*

Tillich's relationship to Buber is illuminated in *Ultimate Concern*, dialogues edited by D. Mackenzie Brown (SCM Press, 1965), and particularly in this address which Tillich gave at a memorial meeting for Buber, not long before his own death. It also sheds interesting light on Tillich himself.

Paul Tillich · *Martin Buber*

It would be inadequate for this occasion if I tried to give a detached evaluation of Martin Buber's work. We are asked to speak here about what he meant to us as a person, as well as in his work. We were asked because one knew that our evaluation of his thought would be, at the same time, a witness and a confession. In this sense I want to speak. And it is in this sense that I shall start with my image of him as a partner in a dialogue which lasted with many interruptions for forty years. It was a dialogue on the basis of our own religious encounters, and it included philosophical as well as theological questions. But first let me tell you about some personal memories.

When less than two years ago I left his home in Jerusalem after a great evening of reminiscences and exchanges, I asked him whether he would come again to Europe or America. He answered with a clear 'No', and he looked at me with an expression in his eyes which said unmistakably: 'This is a final farewell.' It was.

Going back through four decades from this last to our first meeting, I remember the conference of Religious Socialists in Germany in the year 1924. Our movement, founded after the First World War, tried to heal the catastrophic split between the churches and labour in most European countries. It was my task to elaborate adequate concepts from the theological, philosophical and sociological sides. This meant that I had to replace traditional religious terms, including the word 'God', with words which could be accepted by the religious humanists who belonged to our movement. After I had finished, Martin Buber arose and attacked what he called the 'abstract façade' I had built. With great passion, he said that there are some aboriginal words like 'God' which cannot be replaced at all. He was right, and I learned the lesson. I don't believe that concepts like 'ultimate reality' or 'unconditional concern' which are much used in my systematic writing appear in the three volumes of my sermons. This awareness, produced by Martin Buber, enabled me, I believe, to preach at all.

Behind this attack on the conceptual façade of my presentation lay a deeper problem. It came out in two unforgettable evenings of dialogue in the house of mutual friends in New York. At that time both of us were refugees from Nazi Germany. This dialogue was one of the most important I ever had. It dealt with the question how far Buber's I-Thou encounter, contrasted to the I-It relation, is an exact description of what really happens in the encounter of person with person. I asked (in a hidden defence of my conceptual façade many years ago) whether one can say that there is a '*pure* I', related to a '*pure* Thou'. Or whether there is a particular 'I' with qualities, able to be conceptualized, and a particular 'Thou' with qualities, different or opposed, but equally able to be conceptualized; for instance as a male, a European, a Jew of the twentieth century, an intellectual, etc. This question becomes especially important if one asks for the difference between the encounter between man and man, and the encounter between man and God. In order to make this distinction, concepts must be used which are more than façade, and describe the structure of the building itself. But again, what I learned and used later in my ethical writings is the insight that the moral imperative and its unconditional character is identical with the demand that I acknowledge every person as person, every 'thou' as a 'thou', and that I am acknowledged in the same way.

In these dialogues, as in almost all encounters with Martin Buber, something happened which transcended for me in importance the dialogue itself. It was the experience of a man whose whole being was impregnated by the experience of the divine presence. He was, as one could say, 'God-possessed'. God could never become an 'object' in Martin Buber's presence. The certainty of God always preceded the certainty of himself and his world. God, for him, was not an object of doubt, but the presupposition – even of doubt. This is the only way, I believe, which makes a dialogue with those who doubt and even those who deny God, possible. But this presupposes a universalism like that of Martin Buber.

It is characteristic that we never discussed the Jewish-Christian contrast directly. This was not the existential question today for either of us. It was not to be denied, but our real problems could not be discussed in terms of unity and trinity, not even in terms of law and gospel. The reason was that Buber's universalism transcended any particular religion, although it was derived from his interpretation of Judaism, just as I derived my universalism from what I think to be the true nature of Christianity.

This is the reason why our dialogues never were Jewish-Christian dialogues but dialogues about the relation of God, man and nature. They were dialogues between a Jew and a Protestant who had transcended the limits of Judaism as well as of Protestantism, while remaining a Jew the one, and a Protestant the other. This concrete universalism seems to me to be the only justifiable form of universalism.

Martin Buber has been called religiously a prophet, philosophically an existentialist. There is truth and untruth in both statements. He himself resented it to be called a prophet, because he knew that a prophet who calls himself a prophet proves that he is not a prophet. But for those who encountered him, he had prophetic passion and prophetic words. Prophetic means: expressing the divine presence in a particular situation. And that he did. Perhaps he also disliked to be called an existentialist philosopher, but again, he was, even in a very radical sense, as his abstinence from conceptual formulations shows. The existentialist element in his thought was in unity with the prophetic element in his whole being. It was not psychological or sociological existentialism, it was an existentialism rooted in the divine-human encounter. It could be called theonomous, God-determined existentialism.

The intensity of the God experience in Martin Buber had another equally important consequence. He could, without visible conflict, unite the prophetic with the mystical element in the God–man relationship. I consider this union to be the inner aim, the *telos* of the movement of religion and of theological thought. The way he did it was determined by his acquaintance with, and his interpretation of, the Hasidic mystics. This is different from the way in which the main line of Jewish and Christian mysticism tried to create the union of both elements in dependence on Philonic and neo-Platonic mysticism. It was a mystical experience of the divine presence in the encounter and activities of the daily life. Buber knew that the prophetic, without the mystical element, degenerates into legalism and moralism, while the mystical element alone leads to an escape from reality and from the demands of the here and now.

The prophetic as well as the mystical way transcends religion in the narrower sense of the word, without necessarily denying it. This gave Martin Buber his freedom from ritualism and his freedom for the secular world. But, of course, it brought him also suspicion and hostility from those who make a true relation to God dependent on the belonging to a particular religion with particular ritual and doctrinal norms. Buber was open for the cultural creations of past and present, in philosophy as well as the arts, in the social as well as in the political realm. For him, God was present and could be found in the universe of nature and of history. This openness for the secular – in which I always agreed in the name of which I call the Protestant Principle – anticipated an emphasis which has appeared in the latest phase of Protestant theology: the freedom from religion, including the institutions of religion, in the name of that to which religion points. This attitude is a reason for Martin Buber's far-reaching influence on the secular world, and particularly on the younger generation for which the traditional activities and assertions of churches and synagogues have become largely irrelevant. He knew that we cannot produce new symbols at will, but he also knew that we cannot use them as if nothing had happened in history. This makes him a genuine theologian.

As long as I have known Martin Buber, I felt his reality as something which transcends bodily presence or intellectual influence. He was there in the midst of the Western world, a part of it, a power in it, through his person, but also independent of him as an individual being, as a spiritual reality impossible to be overlooked, provoking Yes or No or both. This spiritual reality which was in the man Martin Buber will last for a long time in future history and open up for many that which is above history.

3

ROMAN CATHOLIC THEOLOGY

TWO OF the most impressive books to appear in recent years have been one-volume commentaries on the Bible by Roman Catholic scholars. Each has around fifteen hundred pages: *The Jerome Biblical Commentary* (Geoffrey Chapman, 1968) has American contributors and is edited by Raymond Brown, Joseph Fitzmyer and Roland Murphy; *A New Catholic Commentary on Holy Scripture* (Nelson, 1969) is written mostly by English scholars and is edited by Reginald C. Fuller, Leonard Johnston and Conleth Kearns. Anyone outside the Roman Catholic tradition who had looked into the earlier *Catholic Commentary*, published in 1953, would have found himself in a world virtually cut off from other theological scholarship: primitive theories about inspiration and infallibility, and virtually no reference to non-Catholic writers; the new commentaries are fully international and can hold their ground in any comparison with modern non-Catholic biblical study. Individual scholars have for some time been making reputations in specialist areas; now Catholic research has given a demonstration of all-round brilliance and awareness.

This development in biblical study has come with a more general renaissance in Roman Catholic theology since the Second World War. For long, the tradition was dominated by a 'siege mentality', an introspective concern with the repetition and consolidation of the past teaching of the Church, so that it played virtually no part in the discussion of the problems which were exercising theologians of other communions. Thanks to the improved ecumenical atmosphere of the past two decades, however, discussions have grown up in academic theology between Roman Catholics and Protestants, and these in turn have had considerable influence on theological writing within Roman Catholicism.

Roman Catholic studies on the theology of Barth, Bultmann and Tillich are well known to non-Roman Catholic scholars, as we have already pointed out, but there seems to be some reluctance to study Roman Catholic systematic theologians on their own ground. True, there are difficulties. The chief of these is the context in which theological writing has to be done. While there are many areas of study in which the theologian is free to pursue his own studies where they lead him, there are some – often the most important – where he comes up against the dogmas of an inflexible church authority. At this point he has to be careful about what he says and how he says it. As a result, language tends to grow more complex, footnotes become longer and more frequent, and readability and clarity are lost.

Nevertheless, Roman Catholic theology can no longer be neglected. The three writers represented here may be seen as transitional figures. The stature of Karl Rahner and Eduard Schillebeeckx made them obvious choices, despite the problems of finding representative material. Teilhard de Chardin is an excellent example of the theologian in conflict with his church. A convenient and comprehensive selection of recent Roman Catholic theology may be found in *Modern Catholic Thinkers*, ed. A. R. Caponigri (Burns and Oates, 1960); the famous 'Dutch Catechism', published in English as *A New Catechism* (Burns and Oates, 1967) is a good introduction to a radical, modern approach. Of the more popular English writers, Rosemary Haughton, *On Trying to be Human* and *The Transformation of Man* (Geoffrey Chapman, 1966, 1967), is a very readable example.

What has Roman Catholic theology to offer? If the two future tasks of theology are, as a contributor to the final section puts it, to search for a 'post-Copernican natural theology' and to continue a 'sensitive and lively confrontation' with the Christian tradition, then it has two great strengths. Roman Catholicism has never known the profound distrust of philosophy, metaphysics and natural theology which has characterized much of Protestant theology since the Reformation, and it has always had a positive attitude to the use of reason.

But further progress is still necessary before these potentialities are fully realized. It is still by no means clear that the extent of the problem of epistemology and its consequences for natural theology has come to Roman Catholic theology, and if it is rich in tradition, there are obviously questions about the criteria for interpreting (and criticizing) that tradition which are as yet far from being answered.

Karl Rahner, S.J. (b. 1904), teaches theology at the University of Innsbruck. Most of his theology has been written in the form of long, probing essays which are collected in his *Theological Investigations* (Darton, Longman and Todd, 1961 ff.). But he has also edited Denzinger's classic manual *Enchiridion Symbolorum* and a multi-volume German theological Lexicon. Most recently, he has produced with a colleague a *Concise Theological Dictionary* (Herder–Burns and Oates, 1965), from which the following extracts are taken. They show well the two poles between which his theology moves: along with a re-presentation of the traditional teaching of the Church one can see the influence of existentialist philosophy which marks him out as a pupil of Martin Heidegger.

Karl Rahner · *God, Jesus Christ, Nature and Grace, Philosophy and Theology*

God is the name for him who reveals himself in the Old Testament as unbounded (Isa. 6; 1 Kings 8.27), the incomparable (Ps. 139. 7-12 and *passim*), radically alive (Ps. 90), the absolute master of being (Ex. 3. 13 f.), whose omnipotence is not proved in the abstract but historically by the mighty deeds he has done for his people Israel before the gentiles, who shows himself beyond all doubt to be personal by his loving choice of the people of the Covenant and of the individual. Jesus acknowledges this same God as his Father, who has graciously forgiven and accepted man in Jesus and in Jesus has granted him access to his kingdom. Of his nature he is invisible (Rom. 1.20; John 1.18; 6.46), known only to the Son (John 1.18 and *passim*), but he is recognized as love by his self-communication to the Son and through the Son to the brethren (John 4.16 f.), and finally he has become visible in Jesus, his true image (II Cor. 4.4; Col. 1.15). Christian philosophy and theology conceive God in terms of the analogy of being as absolutely holy, supreme, exalted above the world, personal, absolutely necessary, uncaused, existing of himself, and therefore the eternal and infinitely perfect being, who has created everything else out of nothing.

1. Since God exists absolutely of himself he cannot be called 'being' in the same sense as created being. Being can be attributed to him *simpliciter* and absolutely (*esse ipsum subsistens*) since he possesses the principle of his existence in himself, that is in his own nature; whereas created being only possesses being as derived from God and therefore is only being by analogy. Because God is absolute being in eternal self-possession he can neither be limited nor 'added to'; no unrealized positive potentiality is to be found in him, he is pure act. God's absolute spirituality is grounded in this absolute, original, unlimited self-possession. Though reason can know God through the world which resembles him, 'concluding' from our multifarious experience of the abiding contingency of this experience itself to the principle (cause) of this contingent reality, yet God in his infinity, his absolute perfection and his absolute otherness is incomprehensible for this same finite human thought because God's infinity cannot be grasped in itself or understood in the light of anything else, but being the principle of all understanding remains unfathomable, never entering the realm of human knowledge as an 'object' (only after the manner of an object). Thus he remains the absolute, insoluble mystery and must be thought of as such if God is to remain HE for us. As such, God is the principle and the goal of the transcendental movement of the finite human spirit which is open to the infinite, and the affirmation of God is

always (if unthematically) included in the operations of that spirit (knowing and willing). Since God is given to man as this kind of mystery and nevertheless is considered to be accessible to natural human knowledge, that reason to which the dogmatic definition of the First Vatican Council refers must be understood to mean the capacity for openness to the mystery; but in that case all positive analogical statements about God the infinite mystery will only be understood aright if they are interpreted, in absolute union with their positive content, as referring us to the unutterable mystery and at the same time as protecting that mystery from violation.

2. In actual human life this statement about God owes neither its content nor its incisive force solely to metaphysical knowledge of God derived from the world at large. For this very statement is in part an effect of medicinal grace and an affirmation of faith, that is, it derives from God's self-revelation in history and is realized as faith. Indeed the Church expressly emphasizes how vulnerable, how liable to distortion a purely 'metaphysical' knowledge of God, unsupported by grace and revelation, is in this present world. Our statement, then, should always be understood in the light of our experience of Jesus Christ acting in saving history and grace, so that we shall always say that HE is God. Our ultimate and adequate affirmation of faith therefore will not be, 'There is a God', but: 'This being with whom we have to do in the history of Jesus Christ, who appears there, who reveals and communicates himself as the Trinity, is God, is the only God, the principle of total, multifarious, mutually conflicting reality, is utter Mystery.' Consequently all the (above) abstract metaphysical statements about God in dogmatic theology do not refer to an abstract metaphysical subject but are always an acknowledgment that in our history we have concrete dealings with him of whom we predicate these unutterable things, that we predicate them of him because in our history this is what he shows himself to be like, he whom we are permitted to call THOU.

3. The more particular purpose of this specifically dogmatic affirmation which faith makes about God is thus to declare

him in his absolute uniqueness and hence to infer the absolute obligation of faith in this God of the revelation that has occurred in Christ: God is the being who keeps himself absolutely and essentially distinct from the world, although he is the abiding, all-pervading principle and ground of the world, conserving all things in their own being. He cannot therefore be conceived in pantheist fashion as a personification of the sum of all reality. There is only one such reality, not a quality of this world but existing absolutely in and of itself; it is absolutely 'simple' precisely because of the infinite plenitude of its being, which shares no dimensions with any other entity and therefore is not referred to anything else (simplicity of God). This one and unique reality is described as the 'totality of infinite perfection' (omnipotence, omniscience, etc.). Only the divine incomprehensibility can offer any theological elucidation of this infinitude of perfection. Since an entity can never outstrip its first cause but must rather be eminently contained in the latter, spirit, will, self-consciousness, life must reach their acme in that unique, absolute reality that is God. God therefore is ('*intellectu et voluntate infinitus*') the absolutely free, living, personal God, who has imparted himself to man in saving history, through Christ, in this same plenitude and in impenitent love.

Jesus Christ

The deepest meaning of the life of Jesus lies in what he himself is and what he progressively reveals about himself. He knows that he is truly a human being, a worshipper before God to whose incomprehensible will he submits himself, exposed to everything that is implied in human destiny. But he also knows and declares that he is the Son of the Father as no other human being is – in a sense quite peculiar to himself. He knows that all men's eternal destiny is decided by him because in the last analysis whatever men do they do for or against him. He has power to forgive sins, which God alone can do. He knows he is Lord of the divine law, the Lord and Head of God's Church, the Judge of world history, the Lord of the angels, the only begotten Son who alone knows the Father and whose own nature is the secret of the Father alone. He knows that his place is at the right hand of the Father. Jesus' statements about himself in the Fourth Gospel are indeed – like St Paul's Christology – formulated differently, in more metaphysical terms than in the Synoptics; but they do not materially add to what Jesus says of himself in those first three Gospels. . . .

Thus the mystery of Jesus consists in the fact that he truly stands on both sides of the boundary separating God from creatures: he is the Son of God and the Son of Man. If human nature is conceived as an active transcendence towards the absolute being of God, a transcendence that is open and must be personally realized, then the Incarnation can be regarded as the (free, gratuitous, unique) supreme fulfilment of what is meant by 'human being'. Christ's 'humanity' can be seen as that which results when God in his Word literally becomes other to himself in a creature. In this way Jesus Christ is the summit of creation, the Lord and Head of the human race because he is one of its members, the Mediator between God and creatures. Because Jesus cannot be conceived as man without the world for his environment, God's gracious will for that whole world has become historically concrete, definitely real, in the world; God's decisive and final word, in his dialogue with the world that he has established in freedom, has already been uttered in his Word made flesh. The dignity of the divine Person invests Jesus' moral acts with infinite significance. His obedience, realized in complete surrender to the Father through his death, which he undergoes as head of the human race, is the redemption of the world.

He who hears and believes the message of Jesus and has faith in him, comprehends the fact that God in his sovereign freedom has willed not merely to endow creatures with a genuine freedom *vis-à-vis* the Creator, but also to summon all creation to a share in his very own life in glory by way of the historical life his own Word has lived in the world, in the totality of body and spirit, as the very being of the Word. The Christian believes that this event, on which the final and ultimate salvation of the world depends, has occurred precisely in Jesus of Nazareth, that consequently his doctrine and his spirit are absolute truth and life for men, his death their redemption; that the consummation of the world consists in the definitive revelation of this utter intimacy between God and his creature.

Many a man who rejects the formulae of theological Christology because he understands them amiss may yet existentially have a perfectly genuine Christian faith in the Incarnation of the Word of God. Anyone who contemplating Jesus, his cross and death, really believes that here the living God has spoken to him the final decisive, irrevocable word that delivers him from all bondage to the existential categories of his imprisoned, sinful, death-doomed existence, believes in the reality of the Jesus of Christian faith, believes in the Incarnation of God's Word, whether or not he realizes the fact. To say this, of course, is not to deny the importance of these formulae, which are objectively correct and which provide the sociological basis for community of thought and belief in the Church.

Indeed, many a man has encountered Jesus Christ unawares, laid hold without knowing it on someone into whose life and death he plunged as into his blessed, redeeming destiny. The grace of God and the grace of Christ are everywhere as the secret essence of all that is open to choice, so that it is difficult to grasp at anything without having to do with God and Jesus Christ in one way or another. Any man, therefore, however far he may be from the explicit verbal formulae of any revelation, who accepts his own existence – that is, his humanity – in mute patience (or rather in faith, hope and love, whatever he may call these) as the mystery that conceals within itself the mystery of eternal love and bears life in the bosom of death, says Yes to something which corresponds to his limitless surrender to it, because God in fact has filled it with the limitless, that is with his divine self, when the Word became flesh; though he may not know it, such a one says Yes to Jesus Christ. After all a man who lets go and jumps, falls into the abyss that is there, not only as far as he has plumbed it. To accept and assume one's human condition without reserve (and just who does so remains obscure) is to accept the

Son of Man, because in him God has accepted and assumed man. If Scripture declares that he who loves his neighbour has fulfilled the law, this is the ultimate truth for the reason that God himself has become this neighbour, so that whenever we accept and love our neighbour we are at the same time accepting and loving that one Neighbour who is nearest of all to us and farthest of all from us.

Nature and Grace

Because of its transcendence (*Potentia obedientialis*) the open nature of man is a possible recipient of God's own free self-communication in grace and the beatific vision. Since this transcendence of man, making him capable of objective knowledge and personal freedom, would be intelligible even if the offer of this divine self-communication had not occurred, it is not, even in the concrete human nature that exists, the inevitable consequence of God's act in creating the intelligible being 'man', but a free grace, in no way 'due' to man, even if we abstract from the sin whereby man made himself positively unworthy of this divine gift. Human nature is called 'pure' or mere nature (*natura pura*) when conceived of in a hypothetical order of things where God's self-gift would not be the whole purpose of creation. This conception, it is true, includes the doctrine that grace is absolutely gratuitous even antecedent to sin, but does not suggest that nature as such ever existed nor that what we know from our existential experience of ourselves can be identified with 'pure nature'. In concrete creation, rather, human nature is always summoned to grace and required to accept God's offer of himself, in which alone it finds its real goal, without which it is *ipso facto* in a state of wretchedness; indeed it is created only because God in his ecstatic love is thereby enabled to communicate himself absolutely to that which is not God. Where man culpably rejects God's offer he is not preserving his nature but corrupting it. It then remains not a pure nature but a potential recipient of God's forgiving grace and a nature that has offended against itself, because human nature is precisely man's unqualified, dialogical availability to God.

Philosophy and Theology

The fundamental problem of the relation between philosophy and theology is whether and how they can simultaneously be basic sciences (that is, shed light on being in general and existence in a reflexive, systematic way) in such a way that man need neither abandon, nor sacrifice the character of, either discipline, that is, be faced with the choice of being either a philosopher or a theologian. In order to elucidate this problem we must first observe that Catholic theology draws an essential distinction between nature and grace, and consequently between natural knowledge of God and revelation; so that by its very nature it does not simply tolerate philosophy but actually needs it. That is to say, Catholic theology does not raise the structure of revelation and faith upon the ruins of the human intellect, sinner though man be. Furthermore, history shows that theology has always thought in philosophical terms, among others; and against Modernism and all religion of feeling, Catholic theology holds tenaciously to the historical fact that from the outset revelation and grace address the whole man, not least his intellect – a pertinent fact when one is considering the nature of religion. The Christian believer as such lives in the conviction that intellect, nature and history are the creation, revelation, and property of the God who is the one truth, the source of all being and truth, and has produced historical, verbal revelation to perfect and exalt his creation. The fact, then, that a thing lies 'outside' a particular sphere of earthly reality (in this case outside historical revelation, the Church and theology) by no means removes it from God's domain so far as the Christian is concerned. So that it is neither necessary nor permissible for him to make a closed and final system of theology at the expense of philosophy. To do so would be to confuse theology with theology's God. The Christian above all knows that there is a pluralism in the world which can be positively and adequately unified by no one (except God), not even by the Church and her theologians, though of course there is no question of a double truth. Conversely, if philosophy is to accomplish the intellectual mastery of human existence as it actually is in all its breadth and depth, even the philosopher with the most transcendental approach must take notice of the history of the mind, then it may not ignore the phenomenon of religion, because religion is part of the basic structures of human existence (even where atheism is preached as the true interpretation of life, and therefore as a 'religion'). A philosophy which was not also a 'philosophy of religion' and a 'natural theology', in whatever form would be a bad philosophy, because it would fail to perceive its own object. (A contented atheism which behaves as though the question of religion did not exist either does not know what we mean by God or else is transparent escapism from God and a pose.)

The following considerations are decisive:

1. If philosophy wishes to be systematic, transcendental reflexion (and to the extent that it does), of itself it does not wish to (and cannot) advance any claim to be the concrete, adequate, salvific interpretation of life and thus to substitute itself for concrete, historical religion (and therefore the theology of religion). Should philosophy attempt to be more than such transcendental reflexion ('mediation'), in other words should it attempt to be the concrete maieutic to concrete existence, which always eludes reflex comprehension yet is inescapable and obligatory, and thus to mediate concrete religion, it would have united both theology and philosophy, reason and revelation, under the title of philosophy (or else it would be false, i.e. for the greater part secularized, theology). This would raise a problem of terminology, and analysis would show that this single global grasp of existence falls apart into the familiar elements of reason and revelation, theology and philosophy, which do not allow of being unified by reflexion. But if philosophy, in accordance with its whole tradition, regards itself as transcendental reflexion, then it must be said that such reflexion can never wholly exhaust the concrete reality of existence, though the concrete itself is experienced as the ground of existence, and not its unimportant remainder: historicity is less than real history, concrete love more (not less) than the formal analysis of subjectivity (the ability and the duty to love), the anguish that is experienced is

more (not less) than the concept of this basic condition of human existence. But if this self-limitation of philosophy is one of its basic affirmations in that philosophy is a 'first' (fundamental) science, acknowledging reality as greater than itself but no other science as the source of its principles, then philosophy – being the study of the transcendence of mind and spirit – points to God who is absolute mystery 'in person', constitutes man the potential (it may be) 'hearer of the word' of this living God (perhaps even under the influence of the supernatural existential) through its anthropology and philosophy of religion, and as mere reflexivity and incomplete mediation refers man, who mediates himself historically, to history itself as the locus of his self-achievement. Of itself, therefore, philosophy is not the fundamental science in the sense of claiming that it alone illuminates and masters concrete human existence. When philosophy rightly understands itself and its freedom (liberated by the secret grace of God) it is that first reflex illumination of existence which gives man the courage to take concrete reality and history seriously. But thereby philosophy opens the door to man's discovery in concrete history of the living God who has 'mediated' himself to man through the Incarnation.

2. It is true that in one sense concrete revelation and the Church claim (necessarily, considering their nature) to represent the whole of reality (as its highest principle and its salvation). Hence the Christian, because he is already a believer and has already organized and unified his life in the light of faith, cannot hold that the Church and her doctrine are irrelevant to his philosophy and have no authority over him as a philosopher. Catholic doctrine, if not a material source of his philosophy, is at least a 'negative norm'. However – given the abiding diversity of philosophy and theology which theology itself demands – it does not follow by any means that a Catholic philosopher or theologian must always be able to perceive a positive synthesis between the two disciplines, that is one that is experienced by historical man. The ultimate unity of philosophy and theology may and must be left to the God of philosophy and theology, who is greater than either.

Existentialist influence is even more marked in this passage from the Dutch theologian **Eduard Schillebeeckx, O.P.** (b. 1914), who teaches in the University of Nijmegen. It is a summary of the main points of his most important book, *Christ the Sacrament* (Sheed and Ward, 1963); like Karl Rahner, he has also written a good deal of theology in essay form. Those who simply equate Roman Catholic eucharistic doctrine with transubstantiation will find Fr Schillebeeckx's interpretation surprising. It is a particularly good example of a development beyond a way of thinking in terms of substances to one which takes account of the distinctive quality of our knowledge of each other as persons. Note the emphasis on 'encounter'. Behind this passage lies an immense amount of research into the Christian tradition, as can be seen from the full-length studies from which it has been distilled.

Eduard Schillebeeckx · *The Sacraments, An Encounter with God*

The Sacramental Principle of Revelation

It may be true that Rudolf Bultmann's attempt to demythologize the Christian kerygma, that is to abandon its objective character and interpret it existentially, is unacceptable. It is true, nonetheless, that traditional theology has not always brought out clearly enough the distinction between the mere physical presence of the things of nature and the unique character of conscious human reality and human existence. The personal call which the living God addresses to man in his human situation often seems endangered by a reduction of religious life to the impersonal level. And it was precisely in the theology of the sacraments that this kind of approach resulted in treating sacramental life too exclusively as an impersonal cause-effect relationship. This led to the idea that our reception of grace in the sacraments is mainly a passive affair.

Our aim in this present work is to throw some light on the

essential sacramental character of the Church from the standpoint of *intersubjectivity or existential personal encounter*. Religion, after all, is a dialogue between God and man. By his created powers man can reach God only through the medium of his creation as its First Cause. At the utmost, all man can do is arouse only a powerless longing for the person of the living God (in reality, the three Persons) and for the immediacy of an I-Thou relationship with him. But by reason of the gratuitous, saving initiative of the living God, the religious man finds himself in direct converse with his God. In this divine encounter or personal fellowship with God – called saving grace – consists *salvation*. This encounter is, from God's side, *revelation;* from man's side, his *religious response*.

Revelation and religion – or, in other words, the mutual encounter of man, created and situated in history, with the uncreated God – of their very nature create history and hence, in the widest sense of the word, are truly sacramental. We call sacramental every supernatural saving reality which presents itself in our lives historically. God directs what he plans for man through history, and he does it in such a way that his interventions can be recognized by men as divine. God's giving grace to man makes history by revealing itself, and it reveals itself by becoming history.

Precisely because the supernatural saving reality, veiled in historical events, and surrounded by the darkness of mystery, is present to us only in earthly form (*sacramentum*), it demands the revealing word (*verbum*) as the interior aspect of its earthly appearance. Only in and through the prophetic word is the divine dimension of saving history brought to light. 'Word' and 'sacrament' are therefore the fundamental constituents for revelation in the Old Testament as well as in the New and, after this revelation has been brought to an end, for the life of the Church which grows out of it.

Christianity as Personal Communion of Man with the Living God in Christ

The burden of all God's revelation in the Old Testament is

exactly the course of history which results from the alternation between God's constant fidelity and the ever-recurring infidelity of his people. This revelation, then, is accomplished in a dialectical situation: Out of the dialogue struggle between God and his people, in fidelity and infidelity, the concrete content of revelation takes shape. In one way, of course, this arises from a decision of the living God which is completely and sovereignly free. But looked at from the viewpoint of history, this revelation remains the result of a dialogue of acts: between the invitation and proposal of love by God and the personal, loving response or refusal of love by God's people.

Through all the vicissitudes of this history God desires to lead his people in spite of everything to a final and definitive fidelity. This intention of God appears to be a failure – at least for the majority: The Jews reject their Messiah. The revelation which leads up to Christ, then, evolves in history as a dialogue in which God wrestles with human freedom in his desire to save mankind. It is an existential, two-way struggle between God who calls and man who resists – until this God who invites to a faithful love, himself personally responds as true man to this courtship, with a return of love whose fidelity knows no bounds – which does not shrink even from the death of the Cross.

In the man Jesus is realized the fidelity of the covenant in a a twofold way. At last the dialogue which was ever breaking down finds a full and perfect human resonance. In a single person both elements are fulfilled: the invitation, and the reply of perfect fidelity, and in such a way that both the invitation and the response constitute the completed revelation of God.

The man Jesus is not only the one sent by the Holy Trinity, he is also the one called to be the representative of all humanity. He is not only the visible embodiment of God's wooing of man, but also the representation and highest fulfilment of the human response of love to God's courtship. Jesus, the free man, who in his humanity reveals to us the divine invitation of love, is at the same time, as man, the person who in the name of all of us and as our representative accepts this invitation. As head of redeemed humanity, he is in a sense the whole of mankind. That is why it is possible for his sacrifice to be at the same time our redemption. Only by uniting ourselves to the man Jesus does our own personal fidelity to the covenant become possible. Our personal communion with God can only take place, explicitly or implicitly, by an interpersonal relationship with the man Jesus.

Sacramental Encounter with God through Encounter with the Man Jesus

The encounter of man with the invisible God through the medium of the visible embodiment of the love of that same God in a man we call a *sacramental encounter with God.* To be personally addressed by the man Jesus is for the believer personal encounter with God; for God himself, the eternal Logos, is *personally* this man. Whoever touches with faith the hem of Christ's garment is immediately healed. That is why the human interchange, the interpersonal relationship between Jesus and the men he encounters, is the sacrament of their encounter with God. It means grace and redemption for all who in living faith actually come face to face with the man Jesus.

Social intercourse between men, however, occurs through and in bodily forms. Spiritual influence on a fellow man requires bodily means of communication; it remains a human activity which must find its bodily expression. Jesus was a real man. He was the Son of God appearing in a truly human form, an incarnated human spirit. His contacts with other men required, as do every man's, bodily means of communication. Nevertheless, the encounter of Christ with his fellow men and his properly human activity remain a personal deed of the Son of God, although in human form. It is consequently a divine encounter with men in a truly human form. And as the activity of the Son of God, this encounter of Christ as man with men possesses divine saving power; it is the friendship of God himself for man, translated and transformed into the form of human encounter. Although this is true of every truly human activity of Christ, it is especially true of those human actions of Christ which are exclusively actions of God, although accomplished in a human manner, that is, his miracles and, more especially, redemption itself which finds its consummation in the sacrifice of the Cross.

But since the translation of God's encounter with man into an encounter between men includes bodily elements making it visible, this human encounter of Christ with his fellow men possesses not only *divine* saving power in a very general way (since it is a personal action of the Son of God) but divine saving power which is specifically *sacramental*; for the human actions of Jesus in their visibility and corporality are the human outward manifestation of the divine bestowal of grace. They are 'signs and causes' of grace, and this in such fashion that the same reality which is externally visible (the sign) is the inner saving power itself in visible form: the concrete embodiment of the offering of grace.

That the human actions of Jesus have sacramental saving efficacy in themselves means, finally, that our 'body-spirit' encounter with the man Jesus is the sacrament of our encounter with God. And because redemption through the man Jesus is achieved 'once and for all', and in such a way that every communication of grace remains essentially bound up with this man, therefore, every bestowal of grace or encounter with God will come about in an encounter with this man Jesus. The intersubjective relationship of the believer with Christ, the primordial sacrament, remains the basic event of the Christian religion as personal communion with the three divine persons.

Sacramental Encounter with Christ as the Full Development of Religious Encounter with God

In the appearance of the man Christ, the anonymity of the living God is removed. The man Jesus shows us the true face of the living God in such a way that the universal religious themes come to the fore only in Christ. For in fact God reveals himself not only interiorly through his mysterious appeal to our souls (the impulse of the Holy Spirit drawing us to belief); he has, as we have said, concretized his inner invitation to personal communion with him in saving history and (fully at last) in the human appearance of Christ in this world. God desired not only to be God for us, he wanted to be God for us in a *human* way.

For the first time we can fully grasp what sanctifying grace means; how it reveals, on the one hand, God's boundless desire for a personal communion with us, for the man Jesus who longs to befriend us is precisely revelation of God. On the other hand, it also reveals how profoundly meant our human response to that divine love ought to be, for the man Jesus whose devoted, childlike intimacy with his Father remaining faithful even unto death is also, as vicarious realization of our devotion, the highest realization of religious intimacy with the living God which man has ever undertaken.

The bodily manifestation of divine life through Christ's human soul, the Incarnation, also plays a decisive role in solving the mystery of God's anonymity in the world. That its sacramental character makes Christianity the perfect form of religious life can be elucidated from insights into the true nature of man.

The human body is not only the appearance and countenance of the human person who reveals himself, it is also that in which and by which the soul develops into a full-fledged person. To join both ideas together: in and through the body the soul externalizes its process of becoming a person. By going out into the world, the human person gains self-consciousness. It is only in incarnation, becoming-flesh, that personal activity is completed. Thus, embodiment serves as the sign, although a sign that also veils, of the most intimate personal activity.

The point here is that dynamic personality constitutes itself in and through an activity which externalizes itself also in bodily form. In the body the soul presents itself to another. 'What we in encounter call body is that through which we situate ourselves, express ourselves, and make ourselves known; in short, the form of man's being-in-the-world. The person we encounter has this form, but he also is this form.' It is through the body and in the body that human encounter takes place. In virtue of this, human relationships of a spiritual nature, no matter how independent they are in themselves of bodily encounter, nevertheless do attain their high points in such an encounter because in it the spiritual interrelationship is made fully present.

Of course, we should by no means overlook the unique

characteristic of the man Christ. He is truly God-man, divine in a human way and human in a divine way. Nonetheless, he is truly man. What we have said about the human dimension pertains also to Christ in his personal relationships with his fellow men. For the apostles, the moments of their companionship with Christ in both soul and body were the decisive high points of their experience of Christ. The Last Supper is a typical example, or Jesus' glance to Peter after his denial, which was enough to move him to tears.

In such bodily-spiritual encounters Christ himself makes the gift of his presence an intensely vivid reality, while in those also bodily encounters the disciples experience their spiritual bond with Christ more deeply than ever. On both sides the bodily personal encounter is the point at which spiritual encounter culminates. And since the spiritual intervention of the man Jesus, the redeeming God, is an intervention in grace, this means that the sacramentalizing or the embodying of this gracious intervention is the culmination of Christ's will to bestow grace and bring salvation. Conversely, whoever in faith encounters the man Jesus and is offered his mercy in a visible and tangible form can achieve through this a fully developed religious attitude.

In the encounter with Christ the anonymity of man's experience of God is removed. In religions outside of Christianity man cannot normally reach to an experience of God except in a vague and often nameless way. It is only in the sacramental encounter with Christ that this experience of God can develop into a mature and fully personal religious worship. The full unfolding of religious life has, therefore, a sacramental basis: the primordial sacrament, Christ Jesus.

The Sacraments of the Church as Human Encounter with the Glorified Kyrios (Lord)

Must we who have never encountered Christ in the flesh and who have not yet taken up in glory – must we manage to get along meanwhile without bodily encounter with Christ? Must our Christ encounter occur in a purely mystical fashion, in the purely spiritual contact of faith, as our Protestant brothers in the faith suppose? The first answer that suggests itself is: in a certain sense, yes; just as those of the Old Covenant and also the other non-Jewish and non-Christian religions had to and still have to get along without any bodily encounter with Christ, although all of these were and are already indebted to Christ for everything. This makes Catholic life fundamentally a life of waiting: 'Waiting for the blessed hope' (Titus 2.13). Our eschatological eagerness is a vigil, an advance toward a meeting, an encounter not yet complete. Christianity is the religion of Maranatha: 'Come, Lord Jesus!' (Rev. 22.20); 'Thy Kingdom come!' (Matt. 6.10; Luke 11.2).

But this is only one aspect. This active expectation of the perfect encounter is not sustained merely through an encounter with Christ which is only spiritual, or achieved through a mystical act of faith; but it is sustained just as much through an encounter with the living *Kyrios* (Lord) which, though unique, is nevertheless real and quasi-bodily – this encounter takes place in the sacraments of the Church and through them. And this quasi-bodily or strictly sacramental encounter with Christ is for that very reason a pledge and anticipation of the eschatological and perfect encounter with Christ.

From behind the cloud of his glorification, behind which he withdraws from our still earthly eyes, the Lord in his visible Church reaches for earthly, unglorified elements which for that very reason are visible to us, elements as unpretentious as the child in the crib: a little bread and wine, oil and water, a fatherly hand upon the forehead, in order to make his heavenly, saving act effectively present to us here and now. The Church's sacraments are, therefore, our quasi-bodily encounters with the transfigured man Jesus, a veiled contact with the Lord but, nonetheless, one which is concretely human in the full sense because both body and soul are involved. Therefore, based on the historical redemptive event of Christ who is himself the *Eschaton*, the sacramental encounter is a celebration in mystery of the Parousia.

From this we see the 'why' of the Church's sacraments. The man Jesus, the visible, fully human image of the redeeming God, is, as we have said, the 'once-for-all' sacramental sign in which the mystery of the divine redeeming love is visibly represented to us and through which the redeeming God introduces us into existential, personal communion with himself. Since the Ascension has withdrawn the man Jesus from the visible horizon of our lives, our encounter with the living Lord Christ, our perennial mediator, would take place purely mystically by faith if there were no sacraments. Irremediably one of the human dimensions of the Incarnation would in fact be lost for all of us who have never encountered Christ in his earthly life. But God has remained true to his pedagogy. With sympathetic consideration for the characteristic situation of the human person who, because of his bodily nature, lives in a world of men and things, and reaches spiritual maturity in them and through them, God ever offers us the kingdom of Heaven in earthly garb. Thus it was in the days of the covenant; thus it was at the *ephapax* (once and for all) (Heb. 9.12) of the human appearance of the redeeming God; and this is what the divine pedagogy requires now in the sacramental Church which is the earthly, visible instrument of salvation employed by the living, invisible *Kyrios*.

The divine plan of salvation is essentially a sacramental economy of salvation. It is true that the spiritual Christ can meet us and influence our lives outside the sacramental visibility of the Church. Nonetheless, *by reason of his glorified body*, he can only make himself *fully present for us and to us* (and thus exploit his grace-giving approach to the full) by using earthly, untransfigured elements as visible symbols, prolonging and manifesting his invisible, heavenly, saving act. The concrete presence of this heavenly saving activity of Christ demands that the *Kyrios* embody his invisible, saving efficacy in this earthly world by employing unglorified corporality which becomes an interior element of his heavenly, symbolic action. The sacramentalism of the Church bridges the disproportion between our untransfigured world and the Christ: the world, that is, which at one point, at its centre, is already glorified.

In the context of this historical milieu in which we live, the sacraments are a visible expression of the celestial, present, saving action of Christ, the Eschaton. In the sacraments we encounter Christ, though he be bodily absent, in a tangible, bodily way. The Eucharist is for us the crowning point of this actual encounter with Christ.

Thus we see immediately that the so-called *sacramenta separata* (separated sacraments) are not things, but rather personal encounters with the glorified man Jesus and in him with the living God. . . .

The Sacrament as Religious Experience

The inner religious condition of the receiving subject is not merely a disposition which precedes or parallels the sacrament; it enters into the very essence of the fruitful sacrament. Of course, the religious experience contributes in no respect to the *validity* of the sacrament. Christ's demonstration of love has absolute priority over every human response and does not depend on it; rather, this response is supported by Christ's love. However, it remains true that only when some inchoate religious ardour is present in the believer who is to receive the sacrament will his sharing in the mystery of worship of the Church be a worthy sacramental expression of his inner spirit. Then this worthily received sacrament will become not only the worshipping petition of Christ and his Church but also that of the receiver: the sacramental expression of his religious desire for grace and his will to encounter Christ. If such a religious desire for encounter does not exist, the valid sacrament (i.e., Christ's will for encounter in and through his Church) cannot develop into a real mutual encounter. As a personal encounter with the glorified Kyrios, the sacrament which is completely genuine therefore necessarily implies the religious ardour of the receiving subject.

The personal religious dispositions of the receiver (which differ depending on whether we are dealing with a sacrament of the living or of the dead) will, therefore, be sacramentalized *in* the worshipping activity of the Church, which then – solely by virtue of the redemption of Christ – bestows sacramental grace *ex opere operato*, that is, brings about the actual encounter with Christ. From this we see that the sacraments do not work automatically, but rather that, as a result of faith and a deep religious longing, they lay hold of the sanctifying power of Christ which is at work in the sacramental Church. But this grasping of salvation in faith is actually the person's *being grasped* by the redeeming Christ. ('The passion of Christ obtains its effect in those to whom it is applied through *faith and charity* and through the *sacraments of faith.*')

The sacraments are, therefore, no easier path to holiness, as though they could dispense us from a part of that religious striving which is demanded in order to attain the grace of reconciliation or interior intimacy with God outside the sacraments. As we have seen, the significance of sacraments as incarnations of the religious disposition is rather that they bring about *moments of supreme ardour* in the everyday life. In contrast to the extrasacramental communion with God, the sacramental life of grace and love is the full and mature stature of the Christian life. As modern anthropology points out, there are in human life, besides the *decisive* or *momentous* actions in which the person achieves more intensive self-expression, also *everyday* actions in which personal freedom expresses itself in a lesser or more moderate degree. So also there are decisive Christian acts and also everyday acts of grace. Because of their sacramental incarnation, the sacramental acts of worship are intended to be decisive and momentous actions of the Christian life. They demand, therefore, more intensive deliberation and reflection; otherwise they become flat and are reduced to a soulless formalism. On the part of Christ too, the sacraments, as earthly embodiments of his heavenly saving act, are the tangible and complete intervention of his gracious will. Therefore, what is normally experienced as something *ordinary* outside the sacraments should grow in and through the sacraments toward a special crowning experience, toward full and complete maturity.

Thus, the seven sacraments indicate the high points of our Christian existence. They give sharp and clear dimensions to everyday Christian life, which at regular intervals raise up the level of everyday spiritual life to new heights. In them the ordinary day-to-day pattern must once again be left behind and surpassed if it is not to fade into that colourless anonymity which, once sacramental practice is abandoned, leads in time to the surrender of Christianity itself and, finally, of all religious spirit.

The sacraments are God's own saving act as it manifests itself in the sacred realm of the Church, as it concretely addresses man and takes hold of him as perceptibly and visibly as a mother embraces her child. Although the child already realizes that his mother loves him, still the felt embrace gives the experience of love in its fullness. 'Now we truly know.' On our way to Emmaus which leads to the *Eschaton*, the sacrament is the veiled encounter in which our heart, listening with eager and ardent faith, burns within us. 'Were not our hearts burning within us while he spoke to us on the road?' (Luke 24.32). Precisely because of their sacramental character, i.e., because the sacraments are an authentic, visible proof of Christ's desire to give grace to the one who receives them, they give us a tranquil, moral certitude of the reality of this gift of grace – a certitude which is lacking in grace bestowed outside the sacraments. This very fact makes us experience the divine graciousness of redemption even more intensely than the bestowal of grace outside the sacraments.

Pierre Teilhard de Chardin, S.J. (1881-1955), stands apart from present-day Roman Catholic theology, not only because of the subject matter about which he writes, but also because of his Church's uncertainty in recognizing him. Priest, scientist and mystic (Robert Speaight, *Teilhard De Chardin: A Biography*, Collins, 1967, is a full account of his life; Vernon Sproxton, *Teilhard de Chardin*, SCM Press, 1971, is a shorter and more approachable introduction), his writings have had a wide appeal, particularly to those who feel that theologies of the existentialist type fail to do justice to a cosmic dimension in the Christian message. Granted the power of his vision, two questions need to be asked. From the Christian tradition: despite Teilhard's apparent intentions, is his doctrine of God an adequate one, or is it not dangerously near either to pantheism or to the 'developing' God of process philosophy, an idea which raises enormous problems? And from the scientific side: does Teilhard remain true to his assertion that he is simply describing phenomena, or is he not rather doing something more? At this point the questioning passes into the wider issue of the problem of how we know, with which so much of this *Reader* is directly or indirectly concerned. Has Teilhard's theology an answer to the pressures outlined in the next two sections? Does it offer any substantial help there?

Pierre Teilhard de Chardin · *The Essence of the Phenomenon of Man*

1. *A World in Involution or The Cosmic Law of Complexity-Consciousness*

The astronomers have lately been making us familiar with the idea of a universe which for the last few thousand million years has been expanding in galaxies from a sort of primordial atom. This perspective of a world in a state of explosion is still debated, but no physicist would think of rejecting it as being tainted with philosophy or finalism. The reader should keep this example before him when he comes to weigh up the scope, the limitations and the perfect scientific legitimacy of the views I have . . . put forward. Reduced to its ultimate essence, the substance of these long pages can be summed up in this simple affirmation: that if the universe, regarded sidereally, is in process of spatial expansion (from the infinitesimal to the immense), in the same way and still more clearly it presents itself to us, physicochemically, as in process of organic involution upon itself (from the extremely simple to the extremely complex) – and, moreover, this particular involution 'of complexity' is experimentally bound up with a correlative increase in interiorization, that is to say in the psyche or consciousness.

In the narrow domain of our planet (still the only one within the scope of biology) the structural relationship noted here between complexity and consciousness is experimentally incontestable and has always been known. What gives the standpoint taken in this book its originality is the affirmation, at the outset, that the particular property possessed by terrestrial substances – of becoming more vitalized as they become increasingly complex – is only the local manifestation and expression of a trend as universal as (and no doubt even more significant than) those already identified by science: those trends which cause the cosmic layers not only to expand explosively as a wave but also to condense into corpuscles under the action of electro-magnetic and gravitational forces, or perhaps to become dematerialized in radiation: trends which are probably strictly inter-connected, as we shall one day realize.

If that be so, it will be seen that consciousness (defined experimentally as the specific effect of organized complexity) transcends by far the ridiculously narrow limits within which our eyes can directly perceive it.

On the one hand we are logically forced to assume the existence in rudimentary form (in a microscopic, i.e. an infinitely diffuse, state) of some sort of psyche in every corpuscle, even in those (the mega-molecules and below) whose complexity is of such a low or modest order as to render it (the psyche) imperceptible – just as the physicist assumes and can calculate those changes of mass (utterly imperceptible to direct observation) occasioned by slow movement.

On the other hand, there precisely in the world where various physical conditions (temperature, gravity, etc.) prevent complexity reaching a degree involving a perceptible radiation of consciousness, we are led to assume that the involution, temporarily halted, will resume its advance as soon as conditions are favourable.

Regarded along its axis of complexity, the universe is, both on the whole and at each of its points, in a continual tension of organic doubling-back upon itself, and thus of interiorization. Which amounts to saying that, for science, life is always under pressure everywhere; and that where it has succeeded in breaking through in an appreciable degree, nothing will be able to stop it carrying to the uttermost limit the process from which it has sprung.

It is in my opinion necessary to take one's stand in this actively convergent cosmic setting if one wants to depict the phenomenon of man in its proper relief and explain it fully and coherently.

2. *The First Appearance of Man or The Individual Threshold of Reflection*

So as to overcome the improbability of arrangements leading to units of ever-increasing complexity, the involuting universe, considered in its pre-reflective zones, proceeds step by step by dint of billion-fold trial and error. It is this process of groping, combined with the two-fold mechanism or reproduction and heredity (allowing the hoarding and the additive improvement of favourable combinations obtained, without the diminution, indeed with the increase, of the number of individuals engaged), which gives rise to the extraordinary assemblage of living stems forming what I have called the tree of life – though I could equally well have chosen another image, that of the spectrum, in which wave-length would correspond to a particular shade of consciousness or instinct.

From one point of view, the various stems of this psychical fan may seem (indeed they are often so regarded by science) to be vitally equivalent – just so many instincts, so many equally valid solutions to a given problem, comparison between which is futile. A second original point in my position in *The Phenomenon of Man* – apart from the interpretation of life as a universal function of the cosmos – lies, on the contrary, in giving the appearance on the human line of the power of reflection the value of a 'threshold' or a change of state. This affirmation is far from being an unwarranted assumption or based initially on any metaphysics of thought. It is a choice depending experimentally on the curiously underestimated fact that, from the threshold of reflection onwards, we are at what is nothing less than a new form of biological existence, characterized, amongst other peculiarities, by the following properties:

a. The decisive emergence in individual life of factors of internal arrangement (*invention*) above the factors of external arrangement (utilization of the play of chance).

b. The equally decisive appearance between elements of true forces of attraction and repulsion (sympathy and antipathy), replacing the pseudo-attractions and pseudo-repulsions of pre-life or even of the lower forms of life, which we seem to be able to refer back to simple reactions to the curves of space-time in the one case, and of the biosphere in the other.

c. Lastly, the awakening in the consciousness of each particular element (consequent upon its new and revolutionary aptitude for foreseeing the future) of a demand for 'unlimited survival'. That is to say, the passage, for life, from a state of relative irreversibility (the physical impossibility of the cosmic involution to stop, once it has begun) to a state of absolute irreversibility (the radical dynamic incompatibility of a certain prospect of total death with the continuation of an evolution that has become reflective).

These various properties confer on the zoological group possessing them a superiority that is not only quantitative and numerical, but functional and vital – an indisputable superiority, I maintain, provided that we make up our minds to apply relentlessly and to the bitter end the experimental law of Complexity-Consciousness to the global evolution of the entire group.

3. *The Social Phenomenon*
or The Ascent Towards a Collective Threshold of Reflection

As we have seen, from a purely descriptive point of view, man was originally only one of innumerable branches forming the anatomic and psychic ramifications of life. But because this particular stem, or radius, alone among others, has succeeded, thanks to a privileged structure or position, in emerging from instinct into thought, it proves itself capable of spreading out in its turn, with this still completely free zone of the world, so as to form a spectrum of another order – the immense variety of anthropological types known to us. Let us take a glance at this fanning-out. In virtue of the particular form of cosmogenesis adopted here, the problem our existence sets before our science is plainly the following: To what extent and eventually under what form does the human layer still obey (or is exempt from) the forces of cosmic involution which gave it birth?

The answer to the question is vital for our conduct, and depends entirely on the idea we form (or rather ought to form) of the nature of the social phenomenon as we now see it in full impetus around us.

As a matter of intellectual routine and because of the positive difficulty of mastering a process in which we are ourselves swept along, the constantly increasing auto-organization of the human myriad upon itself is still regarded more often than not as a juridical or accidental process only superficially, 'extrinsically', comparable with those of biology. Naturally, it is admitted, mankind has always been increasing, which forces it to make more and more complex arrangements for its members. But these *modus vivendi* must not be confused with genuine ontological progress. From an evolutionary point of view, man has stopped moving, if he ever did move.

And this is where, as a man of science, I feel obliged to make my protest and object.

A certain sort of common sense tells us that with man biological evolution has reached its ceiling: in reflecting upon itself, life has become stationary. But should we not rather say that it leaps forward? Look at the way in which, as mankind technically patterns its multitudes, *pari passu* the psychic tension within it increases, with the consciousness of time and space and the taste for, and power of, discovery. This great event we accept without surprise. Yet how can one fail to recognize this revealing association of technical organization and inward spiritual concentration as the work of the same great force (though in proportions and with a depth hitherto never attained), the very force which brought us into being? How can we fail to see that after rolling us on individually – all of us, you and me – upon our own selves, it is still the same cyclone (only now on the social scale) which is still blowing over our heads, driving us together into a contact which tends to perfect each one of us by linking him organically to each and all of his neighbours?

'Through human socialization, whose specific effect is to involute upon itself the whole bundle of reflexive scales and fibres of the earth, it is the very axis of the cosmic vortex of interiorization which is pursuing its course': replacing and extending the two preliminary postulates stated above (the one concerning the primacy of life in the universe, the other the primacy of reflection in life) this is the third option – the most decisive of all – which completes the definition and clarification of my scientific position as regards the phenomenon of man.

This is not the place to show in detail how easily and coherently this organic interpretation of the social phenomenon explains, or even in some directions allows us to predict, the course of history. Let it be merely stated that, if above the elementary hominization that culminates in each individual, there is really developing above us another hominization, a collective one of the whole species, then it is quite natural to observe, parallel with the socialization of humanity, the same three psycho-biological properties rising upwards on the earth that the individual step to reflection originally produced.

a. Firstly the power in invention, so rapidly intensified at the present time by the rationalized collaboration of all the forces of research that it is already possible to speak of a human rebound of evolution.

b. Next, capacity for attraction (or repulsion), still operating in a chaotic way throughout the world but rising so rapidly around us that (whatever be said to the contrary) economics will soon count for very little in comparison with the ideological and the emotional factors in the arrangement of the world.

c. Lastly and above all, the demand for irreversibility. This emerges from the still somewhat hesitating zone of individual aspirations, so as to find categorical expression in consciousness and through the voice of the species. Categorical in the sense that, if an isolated man can succeed in imagining that it is possible physically or even morally, for him to contemplate a complete suppression of himself – confronted with a total annihilation (or even simply with an insufficient preservation) destined for the fruit of his evolutionary labour – mankind, in its turn, is beginning to realize once and for all that its only course would be to go on strike. For the effort to push the earth forward is much too heavy, and the task threatens to go on much too long, for us to continue to accept it, unless we are to work in what is incorruptible.

These and other assembled pointers seem to me to constitute a serious scientific proof that (in conformity with the universal law of centro-complexity) the zoological group of mankind – far from drifting biologically, under the influence of exaggerated individualism, towards a state of growing granulation; far from turning (through space-travel) to an escape from death by sidereal expansion; or yet again far from simply declining towards a catastrophe or senility – the human group is in fact turning, by planetary arrangement and convergence of all elemental terrestrial reflections, towards a second critical pole of reflection of a collective and higher order; towards a point beyond which (precisely because it is critical) we can see nothing directly, but a point through which we can nevertheless prognosticate the contact between thought, born of involution upon itself of the stuff of the universe, and that transcendent focus we call Omega, the principle which at one and the same time makes this involution irreversible and moves and gathers it in.

4

SCIENCE AND SECULARIZATION

CONTEMPORARY theology has produced many memorable, if not always particularly meaningful, catch-phrases, but the best known of them must be two from the fragmentary remarks at the end of Dietrich Bonhoeffer's *Letters and Papers from Prison* (SCM Press, revised edition, 1967): 'mankind come of age' and 'religionless Christianity'. Far from being meaningless, these words have proved apt descriptions of key points in a debate which has become particularly prominent over the last ten years, about the nature and significance of 'secularization'.

Secularization has been defined in numerous ways, but all these definitions have positive and negative sides which are closely connected with Bonhoeffer's two phrases. Negatively, secularization is seen as a historical process which has been going on in Europe for many centuries and is rapidly spreading to the rest of the world. By this process the world has gradually been 'de-divinized', i.e. numerous areas of life and thought have been withdrawn from religious control and from the jurisdiction of a 'revealed' religious system, with the result that an open society has grown up where, in theory at any rate, no outside pressures are exerted on individuals to conform to any one set of beliefs. With the Church thus becoming to all intents and purposes one institution, and Christianity one way of life, among others, this has inevitably led to its outward decline, like that of other forms of religion.

The positive force which has brought about this process (which can be seen most clearly, because of the more rapid pace of developments and the non-Christian setting, in Africa and Asia today), is a belief in human omni-competence to explain, order and transform man's natural and social environment.

To be found first in the humanities, this belief gathered strength rapidly with the development of modern science and technology, and it is there that it is most clearly exemplified. As alternative explanations have been found to questions which were once thought to be exclusively religious ones, theology has suffered the same fate academically as the Church has in society. For the dominance of a secular outlook calls in question the very existence of anything lying behind the world of human thought and experience. The heavenly Father seems to have been forced out, 'mankind has come of age'.

Between 1965 and 1969 much of the debate over secularization was carried on around the slogan 'God is dead', and the 'Death of God Controversy' inspired titles like T. J. J. Altizer's *The Gospel of Christian Atheism* (Collins, 1967) and *Radical Theology and the Death of God* (with William Hamilton: Penguin Books, 1968), chronicled in William Miller, *Goodbye Jehovah* (Hodder, 1969). What, it was asked, is the future of Christian belief in a world where man is secular and God is no more?

In 1970, the debate now seems more like a hothouse plant, forced too soon and capable of survival only in an artificial temperature. Of course, 'secularization' is a factor very much to be taken into account, and the problem of talking meaningfully about God is a considerable one (see section 5), but the terms in which it has regularly been raised in the past seem to be determined by faulty presuppositions. 'Secular theology' has been remarkably shallow in its analysis of man, and in many cases its maxims about the possibility of belief in God can be traced back to a one-sided interpretation of Bonhoeffer and, behind him, Barth.

The dispute in England between Bryan Wilson, *Religion in Secular Society* (Penguin Books, 1969) and David Martin, *The Sociology of English Religion* (Heinemann Educational, 1967) illustrates some of the factors that need to be taken into account in a sociological analysis; John Macquarrie, *God and Secularity* (Lutterworth, 1968) provides a theological critique.

As Bonhoeffer quite rightly saw, the question behind the whole debate over secularization is nothing less than 'What is Christianity for us today?', and it does not immediately admit of a ready answer. The three extracts which follow will best be seen as three provocative ways of posing the problem without over-simplification. Whatever answer may suggest itself, one thing is quite clear. It will also have to be an answer to the problems which are raised in other parts of this book. More than that, it will have to pay considerably more attention to the findings of sociological and cultural studies than has previously been the case.

Carl-Friedrich von Weizsäcker is not a theologian, but he is particularly well qualified to discuss the history and significance of secularization, and in fact offers a carefully balanced analysis of it. Born in 1912, he had a most distinguished career in physics, establishing the Kant-Laplace nebular theory for the evolution of the planetary system and doing original work in nuclear physics before leaving the Max Planck Institute to take up the chair of Philosophy at Hamburg University, in 1957. His Gifford Lectures on *The Relevance of Science* (Collins, 1964), which end with a discussion of secularization, of which the following is a part, are a penetrating description of the influence of science on modern society.

C. F. von Weizsäcker · *What is Secularization?*

The Concept of Secularization

Let us first remind ourselves of the main stages in the course of these lectures up till now.

I began with the question 'What does science mean for our

time?' In connection with this question, I formulated two theses which I now repeat for reconsideration:

1. Faith in science plays the role of the dominant religion of our time.
2. The relevance of science for our time can, at least today, only be evaluated in concepts which express an ambiguity.

I then proposed, as a limited contribution to the diagnosis of our time, a study of the historical origin of this faith in science. This was to centre on a special example, for which I selected the history of the concepts of creation and cosmogony.

First, I spoke of mythical cosmogonies which were at the same time theogonies. I attempted to show how they united two elements which seem to us to be essentially different: a well-considered narrative of the physical origin of all things and the expression of an understanding of human existence. As the gods changed, so the two aspects of cosmogony changed. The God of the Jews taught his people to make a sharp distinction between good and evil, that is between life and death. Greek philosophy made a distinction between true and false, that is between being and non-being. I attempted to show how the Jewish and Greek ideas of the beginning of the world corresponded to the understanding of life and truth among both peoples. Then Christianity transformed pre-Christian nature: but the world which it had built was again transformed by modern reality. In modern times, scientific research took the place of an interpretation of the world by traditional symbols. I pursued the growth of a scientific cosmogony. This cosmogony ends, if it is expressed with scientific prudence, in open questions. This was evident in the case of the development of life, which we shall not really understand until we can give a better answer to the two questions, 'What is life?' and 'What is physics?' It was evident in the sphere of astronomy, where the infinity of space and time itself became an unsolved question. At the same time, however, we discovered that many people in our time hold quite firm convictions about these open questions, and we had occasion to assume that these convictions of theirs had their roots in their specific understanding of human existence. Precisely in its unresolved questions, cosmogony is evidently still a symbol of the way in which we understand the basic problems of human life. One of these interpretations is faith in science. Have we understood it better at the end of our course than we did before?

In the first lecture, I narrowed the scope of questions to make it more tractable. Now I must take the opposite step of making it more general. I shall no longer be asking about cosmogony, but about that of which it is merely a symbol. I must of necessity go about this generalizing without attempting a proof. History is too complicated to allow the strict proof of general assertions. I venture this generalizing as a diagnostic hypothesis.

I take up the two initial theses and replace them with more special ones:

1. The modern world can largely be understood as the result of a secularization of Christianity.
2. Secularization is an ambiguous word which describes an ambivalent process.

First of all, I must explain the words used in these sentences.

The word 'secularization' derives from the Latin word *saeculum*, which means century. In traditional Christian language, *saeculum* means the time in which we are actually living today, as opposed to God's eternity: hence it also means everything which belongs to this world and which to that extent does not belong directly to God. Secularization was for a long time a juristic concept which designated the transference of ecclesiastical goods into secular hands. Thus men talked of a secularized monastery. In our century many authors have begun to use the word secularization in a more general way as a description of the process by which the modern world has developed. This use of the word implies certain conceptions which I will discuss in detail; I will begin with some negative remarks.

If the modern world is the product of a process of secularization, it is not a religious world in the strict sense of the word. It is neither properly a Christian world nor is it the world of a new religion, replacing Christianity. It would, however, be equally impossible to describe it as a world totally devoid of any relationship with a religious world. A secularized monastery is the same building as before; its rooms still have the structure of monastic cells, a refectory and a chapel, even if they are now used for other purposes. Similarly, the modern world still has the structure of a Christian world; the drawing of the picture is as it were still Christian, even if all the colours have changed, even if black has changed into white and white into black, as in a photographic negative. If this is so, however, the process can only be ambivalent and the concepts in which we express it must necessarily have an ambiguous sound. For the problem is: Are we to stress the Christian structure, or the non-Christian use of it?

After this explanation of the terminology, I will give examples for the new theses.

One example is the origin of modern science, as we encountered it, for example, with Galileo. In the sixth lecture, I asserted that the concept of strict and generally valid laws of nature could hardly have arisen without the Christian concept of creation. Matter in the Platonic sense, which must be 'prevailed upon' by reason, will not obey mathematical laws exactly: matter which God has created from nothing may well strictly follow the rules which its Creator has laid down for it. In this sense I called modern science a legacy, I might even have said a child, of Christianity. But then I had to show how science lost contact with its parental home. Children can experience the death of their parents.

We have already seen in Galileo's conflict with the Church the ambiguity of any concept which describes this process of secularization. Was Galileo right, when he read the greatness of God in the book of nature, in thinking that he was fulfilling God's will that men should read this book? Was the Church right in thinking that this would distract men from the will of God which stands written in the book of redemption? Using the categories of our century we could describe the positions as being equally ambivalent. If we leave aside the violent means which the Church used wrongly, and, in the long run, used unsuccessfully precisely because they were wrong – did the Church want to hinder the progress of knowledge, or did it require a wider field of vision than that of the fanatical specialist?

The concept of infinity offers another example. The majority of pre-Christian world-views knew only of a finite world. For Christian philosophy, the world was similarly finite, but God was infinite. In modern times, the world takes over this attribute of God: infinity becomes secularized. Under this aspect it is most remarkable that our century has begun to doubt the infinity of the world. I believe that in our time a critical examination of secularization is beginning at exactly the same time as secularization is achieving a consistency hitherto unknown.

The Political Revolutions

In order to see the full weight of secularization, however, we should not limit ourselves to theories. Instead we should speak, for example, of politics. . . .

At first glance, the political revolutions of Europe display many differences, and that should not surprise us, as history never repeats itself. I have spoken of the English Puritan revolution of the seventeenth century and of the French *grande révolution* of the eighteenth century. One difference is that the first of the two interpreted its aims in strictly Christian terms, whereas the second even went through a stage of militant opposition to Christianity. These two revolutions were not notably successful: the revolutionary governments collapsed, and in each case an age of restoration followed. As movements akin to them, which were at first sight more successful, I should mention the American revolution of the eighteenth century and the Russian revolution of the twentieth: both erected systems of government which have lasted down to our time. These systems of government again differ from each other; anyone asserting that one was like the other in any essential feature would in fact win little political sympathy either in the western or in the eastern world. Despite everything, however, I regard it as historically true that all these revolutions, and similarly all the political systems which they set up, either immediately, or after several apparently abortive beginnings, have a great deal in common with each other, and I hope to trace just this common element in them. It is the ambivalence intrinsic to modern civilizations which in my view makes it easy for these systems to regard themselves as being so different: each of them allows of opposed interpretations, each of which contains a good deal of truth.

In speaking in this way, I must, however, make my own standpoint quite clear. I belong to the western world. I share the western conception of political freedom and the rights of man. My remarks would be misunderstood were one to find in them a tendency to obliterate differences in approach to questions in which right and wrong is at stake. A decision is necessary, even if we see what is false on our side and what is true on the opposite side. But I fear that we squander the good consequences of such a decision if we allow the necessary decision, once made, to make us blind to the common feature of all modern systems. We are directed to live with one another in *one* world. Just when we rightly and passionately hope that systems hostile to our own will develop to the standards of humanity which we hold to be the only permissible ones, just at this point, we may not identify these standards with our own historical prejudices and with our own highly ambiguous actions. If self-control is a prerequisite of any ordered conduct in human life, those at least who possess the necessary gifts of understanding and factual knowledge ought to exercise this intellectual self-control in their views about the side which they have chosen as their own in the present historical struggle. This attitude is not only a requisite of good taste: there could come moments in which survival depended on our being capable of it.

I am thus putting forward the supposition that revolutions have very much in common. Let me take the slogans of the French Revolution as a starting-point: Freedom, Equality, Brotherhood. If I see it rightly, these words express a common aspiration of all these different revolutionary movements. The distribution of emphasis may have varied. Perhaps Cromwell's Ironsides tried above all to obtrude their understanding of brotherhood, Robespierre's Jacobins their understanding of freedom, and Lenin's Bolsheviks their understanding of equality on their fellow men. But as soon as we take the three concepts as seriously as they deserve, they do not allow of separation. Can we speak of true freedom as long as it rests on the servitude of part of society? If not, freedom also demands equality. Can we maintain equality by brute force? If not, equality rests on brotherhood. Can I honestly call my neighbour my brother if I do not accord him the freedom I claim for myself? If not, brotherhood demands that a fellow man be permitted his freedom.

The Christian Background to the Modern Ambivalence

The brief analysis of the three basic revolutionary concepts which I have just given was, I think, a Christian analysis. In this sense all modern revolutions have sought to realize Christian demands. But why have they then so forgotten their Christian background that in the most recent of these revolutions it has been felt impossible for the same man to be both a Communist and a Christian at the same time?

If I see things correctly, this progressive amnesia on the part of revolutions corresponds to a quite similar forgetfulness on the part of official Christianity . . . The earliest Church was radical, but not in a political sense. As the success of Christianity brought political life within the purview of Christians, there gradually developed the medieval Church, which in a comprehensive, a catholic way embraced both the radical and the conservative elements.

This catholicism did not mean peace: it meant the incessant strife of the opposed tendencies within the Church, and this strife means life. In modern times the strife has torn apart the catholic unity. The Reformation divided the Church into disputing churches, and secularization divided the world into an official Christianity which tends towards pure conservatism and a non-Christian world whose radicalism no longer understands itself in the light of the Gospel.

If we consider in detail the steps which have led here, today's conditions must seem to be the natural consequence of a necessary development. It is to make that quite clear that I have devoted so many lectures to an extremely specialized problem. But if we look back from our present position to the beginnings of Christianity, the result must seem paradoxical, self-contradictory to the point of absurdity. Let me analyse these self-contradictions.

The Church preserves this most revolutionary document of human history, the Gospel, the truth of which is slowly slipping from the consciousness of the citizen of our modern world. As the Church knows that what it preserves is the truth, it allows itself to be led into the attitude which is assumed by all who preserve supreme good against the changing trends of the day: it allows itself to be seduced into conservatism. At least we will hand down uncorrupted to future generations the good with which we have been entrusted! Laudable as this conservative attitude is, the facts of life force it towards a position which is not so very different from the equally laudable and equally inadequate position of the Scribes and Pharisees. And as usual this is seen much more easily from outside than from within. The Christian concept of the Pharisee, applied to the Church itself, might easily be the last Christian concept the modern world forgets.

Even the person who sees this from the inside cannot *ipso facto* alter it. Despite many still wonderful works and achievements of Christians throughout the world, and despite some hectic exertions on the part of church officials to keep pace with modern times, the Church has for several centuries no longer been leading the historical process; it can hardly still follow it. The most profound thought possible within Christian conservatism is therefore probably that the Church should not in any way lead the process of history; indeed it should not even follow it, as this process is self-destructive, or at least alien to the Gospel. Where this voice has a genuine ring we may not ignore it. But I fear that even it expresses only one side of the truth, and not the complete truth. I feel that it too remains within the sphere of ambivalence, and the consequence of an undetected ambivalence in one's own attitude is blindness to the facts.

The modern world, however, is no less blind. Take one more look at the revolution. *La révolution dévore ses enfants.* We know how blind violent insurgents are to what they really achieve.

Did the Ironsides bring brotherhood? Did the Jacobins bring freedom? Did the Bolsheviks bring equality? I give no answer to these questions, not even a negative one, as even this straightforwardness, judged by the later course of history, would probably be an exaggeration. I would, however, ask: Why this ambivalence of revolutions? Has it perhaps something to do with an age-old dilemma, well known from Christian history, that of violence and non-violence?

The aim of the three revolutions of which I have just spoken was a state of society in which rule by force would no longer be necessary, whether this state of society was given the name of the Fifth Monarchy, the Age of Reason or the classless society. But the way taken by the revolution to this supersession of force is, in fact, force. Of course the thoughtful leaders of the revolution will argue that the ruling power can never be overthrown except by force. Here the leaders of the revolution are expressing a well-known conservative view of human nature. In all previous history those men have ruled who were ready and able to defend their rule by force. It is perhaps the most revolutionary idea of revolutions that this need not always be so. This idea derives from Christian eschatology. But is the revolution that fights for this idea the sole power in history that is justified in using force? Or does it thereby sacrifice its aim to the devilry of the means which it regards as necessary?

This dilemma of revolutions seems to me to throw a special light on the thesis of the mutual blindness of Christianity and the modern world. Christianity does not recognize its own concern in revolutions and is thrown on a fruitless defensive. But revolution sees Christianity only as the guardian of what must perish and therefore forfeits the possibility of understanding its own concern with the aid of concepts which reach deeper than those which it can itself offer. I am therefore attempting once again to portray the dilemma here as it has revealed itself in Christian history – which must be regarded as pre-history to modern revolutions.

In Christianity, the relationship between the end and the means is less simple than in its pagan precursors. In Christian terms, paganism divinized human nature and along with it its intrinsic tendency to use force: this can be seen even in so spiritual a creation as Plato's model state and in a form of government as rooted in ethics as that of the Stoic emperors of the second century. Christ completely rejected the divinization of our natural habits. In the coming kingdom of heaven the rule of these demons will be broken. But, asked the following Christian era, how will the kingdom of God come? It does not come through our efforts: it comes of its own power. This thought contains a deep insight into human existence, which finds its application in daily life. If the demons are conquered, they do not succumb to our efforts of will, but to an operation which we can experience only as a gift of grace. This, however, does not in the least dispense us from any exertion of our will at all. Grace is the answer to our longing for grace, and this longing is not in earnest unless it leads to the most determined personal effort. It is a well-known doctrine that man cannot give himself grace but that he can squander the grace that is offered. This is in accord with the teaching of the Fourth Gospel, that judgment takes place in this life. Should things be otherwise in the great course of world history? But what would this mean for world history?

The final victory over the rule of force is the Last Judgment, the Second Coming of Christ. The orthodox Christian teaching was that no human action could influence the time of his Second Coming. In the present span of time, in which we live in this expectation, we should attempt to live as citizens of his coming kingdom. How this was to be done in practice was, however, the question which produced the tension between radical and conservative Christianity, and I expressed the view that this very tension was the driving force of world history in the Christian era. . . .

What is Secularization?

I chose a strong expression for the ambiguities of our time in saying that while the Church was blind to the true nature of modern times, the modern world was equally blind to its own nature. Both are blind to the significance of secularization. I said that the modern world was the result of a secularization of Christianity. That means that the modern world in certain respects is, and in certain respects is not, a Christian world. Contrary to the beliefs of many Christians and all secularists, I tend to the view that the modern world owes its uncanny success to a great extent to its Christian background. If the men who think that Christianity rests on the deepest insight into human nature which has yet been revealed to us in history are right, this view should not surprise us. To repeat it in traditional Christian language: the gods of nature have been vanquished by the God whom Christians call Our Father; therefore man, as God's son, has received power over nature. As he is son and not servant, he is free, and his freedom includes the freedom to act against the will of his Father, the God of love. He can now subject the world to himself, and secularism does precisely this. (In these last sentences I have followed as faithfully as possible Friedrich Gogarten's theology of secularization.)

But these thoughts need expansion. We must go one stage further in their Christian interpretation and then we must consider them once again from the modern side.

It may be helpful for a Christian theologian to imagine secularism as a Christian heresy. According to the theological definition, heresy (*hairesis*) is to take (*hairein*) a partial truth from the whole of the Christian truth and to make this part absolute. A heretic is a Christian, but an erring Christian. Different varieties of secularism select different aspects of Christianity; I will refrain from going into the details of these aspects. All select the truth that this world is to be changed, a truth which Jesus elucidated in his parables by such different examples as that of the grain of mustard-seed growing into a tree in which many birds can build their nests and that of the all-consuming fire. The modern world is a tree in which many birds build their nests, and it is an all-consuming fire. It is, I say once again, ambivalent. But it is heretical, i.e. blind to the other side of the truth, because it is blind to its own ambivalence. Belief in progress is a half-truth. Jesus clearly described the inevitability of ambivalence in the parable of the wheat and tares, which grow together and will only be separated at the end. I have never seen a clearer description of modern times than this growing corn-field, in which the tares unavoidably grow up alongside the wheat. But he who sees the fact of this ambivalence has taken the first step away from it; he is forsaking the error that made him a heretic. Anyone, on the other hand, who does not see the ambiguity has fallen a hopeless victim to it.

Now I must turn the tables once again. It is not sufficient to call secularism a Christian heresy. One usually thinks of a heresy as the selection of part of a recognized totality of truth. The theologian who speaks of heresy is generally convinced that the Church possesses the all-embracing ('catholic') truth. This conception probably does not even describe the celebrated heresies of the past at all accurately. As a rule, the heretics stressed a side of Christianity which the Church had not taken seriously enough. Many of the Church's dogmatic decisions were called forth by heresies, and I think that the best dogmatic decisions of ancient times had a truly paradoxical character because they incorporated a truth brought to light by heresy in a thought-system which was using an apparently contradictory language. Be this as it may, secularization forces us to attempt a new interpretation of the Christian faith. This new interpretation has been going on for centuries, but it is by no means completed.

I have been at pains throughout these lectures to take account of this new interpretation. . . . But my concern was not what is often called in modern theology the 'demythologizing' of Christianity. As I myself have spent the greater part of my life in surroundings influenced more by natural science than by the Church, I feel the battle of demythologizing to have been decided long ago, perhaps in Galileo's days: it only remains for us to be honest in its consequences. Science has come into being and will, to judge by human standards, endure; in face of it there remains only the task of interpreting Christianity in a way credible to a thought schooled in it. I have attempted this task just as many other modern thinkers inside and outside theology have attempted it. What really concerns me is another question. . . .

Modern thought expresses itself most coherently in science.

But we have no occasion to take science itself as an absolute truth. This holds in every detail. It is indeed virtually the most imposing feature of science that it requires of its disciples that they should be ready at every moment to re-examine even the most generally accepted scientific doctrines. The life of true science is a life of constant self-correction. This must be true still more in respect of the scientific attitude to the wide areas of human life in which science, as we know, does not, at least today, have the answer to the burning questions. And how sure are we of the general philosophical background to science?

If the views of secularization advanced here are correct, they give us additional information which at first sight will not lessen our embarrassment. If these views are correct, modern science would not perhaps have been possible without Christianity. In that case, we are evidently moving in a circle. We explain Christianity in concepts which are to be comprehensible to scientific thought; a thought which for its part is found itself to be a product of Christianity. But any thought which has become conscious of the relevance of history must move in a circle of this sort. Today we can reach a stage of consciousness at which the historical naïvety of those who identify their own standpoint with absolute truth must vanish away. Once we have understood this, we are none the worse for it, for no one will be expected to base his judgments on anything but what he can know. We now understand only our task of constant self-correction better than before. If we are philosophers, of course, we shall have a concept of truth which accords with this stage of consciousness.

Dietrich Bonhoeffer read one of von Weizsäcker's earlier books in prison and it made a tremendous impression on him. Indeed, while there are traces of the new direction taken by his thought in *Letters and Papers from Prison* from earlier periods of his life, much of the writing which has made him famous seems to have been stimulated by what he had been reading during his imprisonment. His remarks are, of course, informal – he describes them as 'thinking aloud', and many of them do not stand up to detailed criticism. But, on the other hand, it is their directness and the circumstances under which they were written which have made them so influential.

Behind Bonhoeffer, as we have seen, the figure of Barth looms large, despite the criticisms which Bonhoeffer makes of him. Note the Barthian influence on Bonhoeffer's concept of religion! Unlike Bultmann and Tillich, Bonhoeffer here argues that men no longer ask 'ultimate' questions, and his verdict on existentialism is a negative one. Is he right here? Because he stands close to Karl Barth in his view of God, he can welcome the process of secularization as a 'clearing of the decks for the God of the Bible'. But in so doing does he leave himself with the possibility of justifying his belief in this God in the face of the pressures illustrated in the next section? And does he really come to grips with the question of what is the distinctive life of a Christian in the twentieth century? The details of the 'non-religious interpretation of biblical concepts' are never, in fact, given. Bultmann's remarks in *Jesus Christ and Mythology* (see above) outline such an attempt – in the following extract Bonhoeffer clearly misunderstands what Bultmann is doing.

Bonhoeffer's theology must in any case be studied against the background of his life. Eberhard Bethge, *Dietrich Bonhoeffer* (Collins, 1970) is a basic source document, but Mary Bosanquet, *The Life and Death of Dietrich Bonhoeffer* (Hodder, 1968) will probably be of greater interest to the English reader.

Dietrich Bonhoeffer · *The Non-religious Interpretation of Biblical Concepts*

What is bothering me incessantly is the question what Christianity really is, or indeed who Christ really is, for us today. The time when people could be told everything by means of words, whether theological or pious, is over, and so is the time of inwardness and conscience – and that means the time of religion in general. We are moving towards a completely religionless time; people as they are now simply cannot be religious any more. Even those who honestly describe themselves as 'religious' do not in the least act up to it, and so they presumably mean something quite different by 'religious'. Our whole nineteen-hundred-year-old Christian preaching and theology rest on the 'religious *a priori*' of mankind. 'Christianity' has always been a form – perhaps the true form – of 'religion'. But if one day it becomes clear that this *a priori* does not exist at all, but was a historically conditioned and transient form of human self-expression, and if therefore man becomes radically religionless – and I think that that is already more or less the case (else how is it, for example, that this war, in contrast to all previous ones, is not calling forth any 'religious' reaction?) – what does that mean for 'Christianity'?

It means that the foundation is taken away from the whole of what has up to now been our 'Christianity', and that there remain only a few 'last survivors of the age of chivalry', or a few intellectually dishonest people, on whom we can descend as 'religious'. Are they to be the chosen few? Is it on this dubious group of people that we are to pounce in fervour, pique, or indignation, in order to sell them our goods? Are we to fall upon a few unfortunate people in their hour of need and exercise a sort of religious compulsion on them?

If we do not want to do all that, if our final judgment must be that the western form of Christianity, too, was only a preliminary stage to a complete absence of religion, what kind of situation emerges for us, for the Church? How can Christ become the Lord of the religionless as well? Are there religionless Christians? If religion is only a garment of Christianity – and even this garment has looked very different at different times – then what is a religionless Christianity? Barth, who is the only one to have started along this line of thought, did not carry it to completion, but arrived at a positivism of revelation, which in the last analysis is essentially a restoration. For the religionless working man (or any other man) nothing decisive is gained here.

The questions to be answered would surely be: What do a church, a community, a sermon, a liturgy, a Christian life mean in a religionless world? How do we speak of God without religion, i.e. without the temporally influenced presuppositions of metaphysics, inwardness, and so on? How do we speak (or perhaps we cannot now even 'speak' as we used to) in a 'secular' way about 'God?' In what way are we 'religionless-secular' Christians, in what way are we the ἐκ-κλησία, those who are called forth, not regarding ourselves from a religious point of view as specially favoured, but rather as belonging wholly to the world? In that case Christ is no longer an object of religion, but something quite different, really the Lord of the world. But what does that mean? What is the place of worship and prayer in the absence of religion? Does the secret discipline, or alternatively the difference (which I have suggested to you before) between penultimate and ultimate, take on a new importance here?

I must break off for today, so that the letter can be posted straight away. I will write to you again about it in two days' time. I hope you see more or less what I mean, and that it does not bore you. Good-bye for the present. It is not easy always to write without an echo, and you must excuse me if that makes it something of a monologue.

I find, after all, that I can write a little more. – The Pauline question whether [circumcision] is a condition of justification seems to me in present-day terms to be whether religion is a condition of salvation. Freedom from περιτομή is also freedom from religion. I often ask myself why a 'Christian instinct' often draws me more to the religionless people than to the religious, by which I do not in the least mean with any evangelizing intention, but, I might almost say, 'in brotherhood'. While I am often reluctant to mention God by name to religious people – because that name somehow seems to me here not to ring true, and I feel myself to be slightly dishonest (it is particularly bad when others start to talk in religious jargon; I then dry up almost completely and feel awkward and uncomfortable) – to people with no religion I can on occasion mention him by name quite calmly and as a matter of course. Religious people speak of God when human knowledge (perhaps simply because they are too lazy to think) has come to an end, or when human resources fail – in fact it is always the *deus ex machina* that they bring on to the scene, either for the apparent solution of insoluble problems, or as strength in human failure – always, that is to say, exploiting human weakness or human boundaries. Of necessity, that can go on only till people can by their own strength push these boundaries somewhat further out, so that God becomes superfluous as a *deus ex machina*. I have come to be doubtful of talking about any human boundaries (is even death, which people now hardly fear, and is sin, which they now hardly understand, still a genuine boundary today?). It always seems to me that we are trying anxiously in this way to reserve some space for God; I should like to speak of God not on the boundaries but at the centre, not in weakness but in strength; and therefore not in death and guilt but in man's life and goodness. As to the boundaries, it seems to me better to be silent and leave the insoluble unsolved. Belief in the resurrection is *not* the 'solution' of the problem of death. God's 'beyond' is not the beyond of our cognitive faculties. The transcendence of epistemological theory has nothing to do with the transcendence of God. God is beyond in the midst of our life. The church stands, not at the boundaries where human powers give out, but in the middle of the village. That is how it is in the Old Testament, and in this sense we still read the New Testament far too little in the light of the Old. How this religionless Christianity looks, what form it takes, is something that I am thinking about a great deal, and I shall be writing to you again about it soon. It may be that on us in particular, midway between East and West, there will fall a heavy responsibility. . . .

The movement that began about the thirteenth century (I am not going to get involved in any argument about the exact date) towards the autonomy of man (in which I should include the discovery of the laws by which the world lives and deals with itself in science, social and political matters, art, ethics, and religion) has in our time reached a certain completion. Man has learnt to deal with himself in all questions of importance without recourse to God as a working hypothesis. In questions of science, art, and ethics this has become an understood thing at which one now hardly dares to tilt. But for the last hundred years or so it has also become increasingly true of religious questions; it is becoming evident that everything gets along without 'God' – and, in fact, just as well as before. As in the scientific field, so in human affairs generally, 'God' is being pushed more and more out of life, losing more and more ground.

Roman Catholic and Protestant historians agree that it is in this development that the great defection from God, from Christ, is to be seen; and the more they claim and play off God and Christ against it, the more the development considers itself to be anti-Christian. The world that has become conscious of itself and the laws that govern its own existence has grown self-confident in what seems to us to be an uncanny way. False developments and failures do not make the world doubt the necessity of the course that it is taking, or of its development; they are accepted with fortitude and detachment as part of the bargain, and even an event like the present war is no exception. Christian apologetic has taken the most varied forms of opposition to this self-assurance. Efforts are made to prove to a world thus come of age that it cannot live without the tutelage of 'God'. Even though there has been surrender on all secular problems, there still remain the so-called 'ultimate questions' – death, guilt – to which only 'God' can give an answer, and because of which we need God and the Church and the pastor. So we live, in some degree, on these so-called ultimate questions of humanity. But what if one day they no longer exist as such, if they too can be answered 'without God'? Of course, we now have the secularized offshoots of Christian theology, namely existentialist philosophy and the psychotherapists, who demonstrate to secure, contented, and happy mankind that it is really unhappy and desperate and simply unwilling to admit that it is in a predicament about which it knows nothing, and from which only they can rescue it. Wherever there is health, strength, security, simplicity, they scent luscious fruit to gnaw at or to lay their pernicious eggs in. They set themselves to drive people to inward despair, and then the game is in their hands. That is secularized methodism. And whom does it touch? A small number of intellectuals, of degenerates of people, who regard themselves as the most important people in the world, and who therefore like to busy themselves with themselves. The ordinary man, who spends his everyday life at work and with his family, and of course with all kinds of diversions, is not affected. He has neither the time nor the inclination to concern himself with his existential despair, or to regard his perhaps modest share of happiness as a trial, a trouble, or a calamity.

The attack by Christian apologetic on the adulthood of the world I consider to be in the first place pointless, in the second place ignoble, and in the third place unchristian. Pointless, because it seems to me like an attempt to put a grown-up man back into adolescence, i.e. to make him dependent on things on which he is, in fact, no longer dependent, and thrusting him into problems that are, in fact, no longer problems to him. Ignoble, because it amounts to an attempt to exploit man's weakness for purposes that are alien to him and to which he has not freely assented. Unchristian, because it confuses Christ with one particular stage in man's religiousness, i.e. with a human law. More about this later.

But first, a little more about the historical position. The question is: Christ and the world that has come of age. The weakness of liberal theology was that it conceded to the world the right to determine Christ's place in the world; in the conflict between the Church and the world it accepted the comparatively easy terms of peace that the world dictated. Its strength was that it did not try to put the clock back, and that it genuinely accepted the battle (Troeltsch), even though this ended with its defeat.

Defeat was followed by surrender, and by an attempt to make a completely fresh start based on the fundamentals of the Bible and the Reformation. Heim sought, along pietist and methodist lines, to convince the individual man that he was faced with the alternative 'despair or Jesus'. He gained 'hearts'.

Althaus (carrying forward the modern and positive line with a strong confessional emphasis) tried to wring from the world a place for Lutheran teaching (ministry) and Lutheran worship, and otherwise left the world to its own devices. Tillich set out to interpret the evolution of the world (against its will) in a religious sense – to give it its shape through religion. That was very brave of him, but the world unseated him and went on by itself; he, too, sought to understand the world better than it understood itself; but it felt that it was completely misunderstood, and rejected the imputation. (Of course, the world *must* be understood better than it understands itself, but not 'religiously' as the religious socialists wanted.) Barth was the first to realize the mistake that all these attempts (which were all, in fact, still sailing, though unintentionally, in the channel of liberal theology) were making in leaving clear a space for religion in the world or against the world.

He brought in against religion the God of Jesus Christ, '*pneuma* against *sarx*'. That remains his greatest service (his *Letter to the Romans*, second edition, in spite of all the neo-Kantian egg-shells). Through his later dogmatics, he enabled the Church to effect this distinction, in principle, all along the line. It was not in ethics, as is often said, that he subsequently failed – his ethical observations, as far as they exist, are just as important as his dogmatic ones; it was that in the non-religious interpretation of theological concepts he gave no concrete guidance, either in dogmatics or in ethics. There lies his limitation, and because of it his theology of revelation has become positivist, a 'positivism of revelation', as I put it.

The Confessing Church has now largely forgotten all about the Barthian approach, and has lapsed from positivism into conservative restoration. The important thing about that Church is that it carries on the great concepts of Christian theology; but it seems as if doing this is gradually just about exhausting it. It is true that there are in those concepts the elements of genuine prophecy (among them two things that you mention: the claim to truth, and mercy) and of genuine worship; and to that extent the Confessing Church gets only attention, hearing, and rejection. But both of them remain undeveloped and remote, because there is no interpretation of them.

Those who, like e.g. Schütz or the Oxford Group or the Berneucheners, miss the 'movement' and the 'life', are dangerous reactionaries; they are reactionary because they go right back behind the approach of the theology of revelation and seek for 'religious' renewal. They simply have not yet understood the problem at all, and their talk is entirely beside the point. There is no future for them (though the Oxford people would have the best chance if they were not so completely without biblical substance).

Bultmann seems to have somehow felt Barth's limitations, but he misconstrues them in the sense of liberal theology, and so goes off into the typical liberal process of reduction (the 'mythological' elements of Christianity are dropped, and Christianity is reduced to its 'essence'). My view is that the full content, including the 'mythological' concepts, must be kept – the New Testament is not a mythological clothing of a universal truth; this mythology (resurrection, etc.) is the thing itself – but the concepts must be interpreted in such a way as not to make religion a precondition of faith (cf. Paul and circumcision). Only in that way, I think, will liberal theology be overcome (and even Barth is still influenced by it, though negatively) and at the same time its question be genuinely taken up and answered (as is *not* the case in the Confessing Church's positivism of revelation!).

Thus the world's coming of age is no longer an occasion for polemics and apologetics, but is now really better understood than it understands itself, namely on the basis of the gospel and in the light of Christ. . . .

Now I will try to go on with the theological reflections that I broke off not long since. I had been saying that God is being increasingly pushed out of a world that has come of age, out of the spheres of our knowledge and life, and that since Kant he has been relegated to a realm beyond the world of experience.

Theology has on the one hand resisted this development with apologetics, and has taken up arms – in vain – against Darwinism, etc. On the other hand, it has accommodated itself to the development by restricting God to the so-called ultimate questions as a *deux ex machina*; that means that he becomes the answer to life's problems, and the solution of its needs and conflicts. So if anyone has no such difficulties, or if he refuses to go into these things, to allow others to pity him, then either he cannot be open to God; or else he must be shown that he is, in fact, deeply involved in such problems, needs, and conflicts, without admitting or knowing it. If that can be done – and existentialist philosophy and psychotherapy have worked out some quite ingenious methods in that direction – then this man can now be claimed for God, and methodism can celebrate its triumph. But if he cannot be brought to see and admit that his happiness is really an evil, his health sickness, and his vigour despair, the theologian is at his wits' end. It is a case of having to do either with a hardened sinner of a particularly ugly type, or with a man of 'bourgeois complacency', and the one is as far from salvation as the other.

You see, that is the attitude that I am contending against. When Jesus blessed sinners, they were real sinners, but Jesus did not make everyone a sinner first. He called them away from their sin, not into their sin. It is true that encounter with Jesus meant the reversal of all human values. So it was in the conversion of Paul, though in his case the encounter with Jesus preceded the realization of sin. It is true that Jesus cared about people on the fringe of human society, such as harlots and tax-collectors, but never about them alone, for he sought to care about man as such. Never did he question a man's health, vigour, or happiness, regarded in themselves, or regard them as evil fruits; else why should he heal the sick and restore strength to the weak? Jesus claims for himself and the Kingdom of God the whole of human life in all its manifestations. . . .

Now for a few more thoughts on our theme. I am only gradually working my way to the non-religious interpretation of biblical concepts; the job is too big for me to finish just yet.

On the historical side: There is one great development that leads to the world's autonomy. In theology one sees it first in

Lord Herbert of Cherbury, who maintains that reason is sufficient for religious knowledge. In ethics it appears in Montaigne and Bodin with their substitution of rules of life for the commandments. In politics Machiavelli detaches politics from morality in general and founds the doctrine of 'reasons of State'. Later, and very differently from Machiavelli, but tending like him towards the autonomy of human society, comes Grotius, setting up his natural law as international law, which is valid *etsi deus non daretur*, 'even if there were no God'. The philosophers provide the finishing touches: on the one hand we have the deism of Descartes, who holds that the world is a mechanism, running by itself with no interference from God; and on the other hand the pantheism of Spinoza, who says that God is nature. In the last resort, Kant is a deist, and Fichte and Hegel are pantheists. Everywhere the thinking is directed towards the autonomy of man and the world.

(It seems that in the natural sciences the process begins with Nicolas of Cusa and Giordano Bruno and their 'heretical' doctrine of the infinity of the universe. The classical *cosmos* was finite, like the created world of the middle ages. An infinite universe, however it may be conceived, is self-subsisting, *etsi deus non daretur*. It is true that modern physics is not as sure as it was about the infinity of the universe, but it has not gone back to the earlier conceptions of its finitude.)

God as a working hypothesis in morals, politics, or science has been surmounted and abolished; and the same thing has happened in philosophy and religion (Feuerbach!). For the sake of intellectual honesty, that working hypothesis should be dropped, or as far as possible eliminated. A scientist or physician who sets out to edify is a hybrid.

Anxious souls will ask what room there is left for God now; and as they know of no answer to the question, they condemn the whole development that has brought them to such straits. I wrote to you before about the various emergency exits that have been contrived; and we ought to add to them the *salto mortale* (death-leap) back into the middle ages. But the principle of the middle ages is heteronomy in the form of clericalism, and a return to that can only be a counsel of despair, and it would be at the cost of intellectual honesty. It is a dream that reminds one of the song *O wüsst ich doch den Weg zurück, den weiten Weg ins Kinderland.*[1] There is no such way—at any rate not if it means deliberately abandoning our mental integrity; the only way is that of Matt. 18.3, i.e. through repentance, through *ultimate* honesty.

And we cannot be honest unless we recognize that we have to live in the world *etsi deus non daretur*. And this is just what we do recognize – before God! God himself compels us to recognize it. So our coming of age leads us to a true recognition of our situation before God. God would have us know that we must live as men who manage our lives without him. The God who is with us is the God who forsakes us (Mark 15.34). The God who lets us live in the world without the working hypothesis of God is the God before whom we stand continually. Before God and with God we live without God. God lets himself be pushed out of the world on to the cross. He is weak and powerless in the world, and that is precisely the way, the only way, in which he is with us and helps us. Matt. 8.17 makes it quite clear that Christ helps us, not by virtue of his omnipotence, but by virtue of his weakness and suffering.

Here is the decisive difference between Christianity and all religions. Man's religiousness makes him look in his distress to the power of God in the world: God is the *deus ex machina*. The Bible directs man to God's powerlessness and suffering; only the suffering God can help. To that extent we may say that the development towards the world's coming of age outlined above, which has done away with a false conception of God, opens up a way of seeing the God of the Bible, who wins power and space in the world by his weakness. This will probably be the starting-point for our 'secular interpretation'.

---

[1] 'Oh if only I knew the way back, the long way back to the land of childhood.'

Cornelis van Peursen is Professor of Philosophy in the University of Leiden. His essay is a convenient example of the way in which the secularization debate is being carried on. Note in particular his positive attitude towards secularization and his stress on 'how things work' to the exclusion of the question of 'how things are'. Is the latter a question which we *can* give up asking? And does Professor Peursen offer an adequate exegesis of the biblical record? A similar approach can be found in Arend van Leeuwen, *Christianity and World History* (Edinburgh House Press, 1964), argued in more detail and at considerably greater length.

Cornelis van Peursen · *Man and Reality – The History of Human Thought*

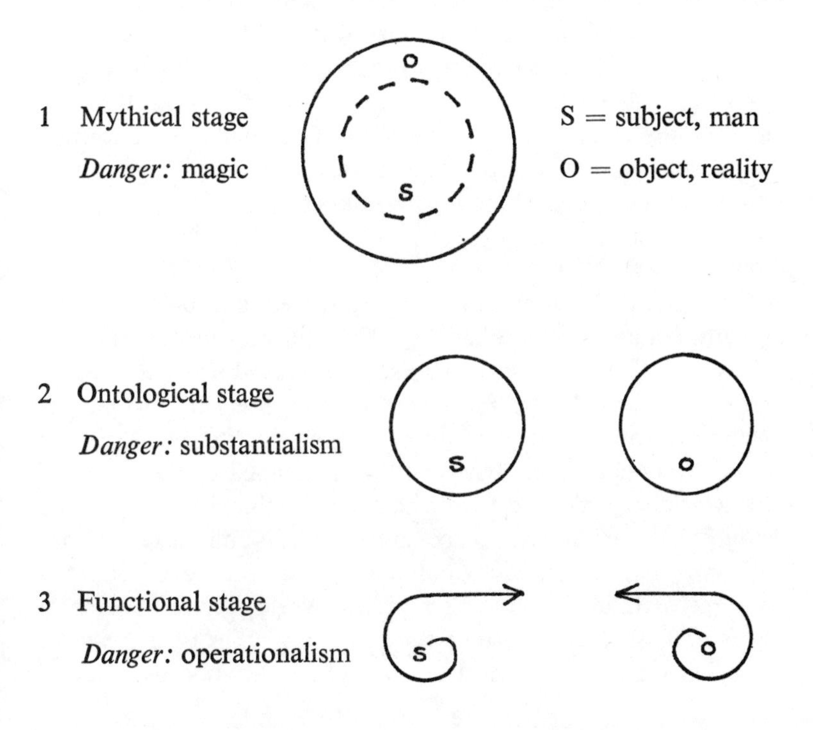

Here is a model showing three stages in the development of reality in the history of human thought. You must not make the mistake of believing that these three stages really represent the development of human thinking. This is only a simplification, a model. A model does not copy reality: it represents reality. It is a kind of scheme, an 'as if'. If the reality were really like this, it would all be rather easy. I shall try to suggest to you that it is rather easy – but in fact it is not! Each of the three stages in the model is implied in the next one: in the second stage you still find features of the first, and in the third are features of the second and first. There will be a fourth stage which cannot yet be known, because we are still in the third. The three stages are ways of thinking; they are kinds of concepts of the world, types of approaches to reality. The first is the stage of myth: this is the period of primitive society. The second is the stage of ontology: of thinking of being as being, and of the rise of society. The third is the stage of functional thinking: the contemporary way of thinking, the contemporary way of life. Each stage has advantages and dangers, and in the long run the dangers become predominant. Each new stage means a liberation from the dangers of the stage that is left behind. This model is concerned only with the main trend, and in fact you never have purely ontological or purely functional thinking.

The Period of Myth

In myth we find man and reality, subject and object, linked together in a rather peculiar way. The subject is merged into the object, is penetrated, so to speak, by reality. For us the real is the super-natural: but for primitive man the real is an overwhelming force. He has as yet no proper identity. He is not yet a well-rounded subject but is still overwhelmed by the forces of the world in which he lives, the social-mythical world. So the subject has not yet taken on concrete shape. Numinous forces are everywhere. Looking back upon that period we speak of 'haunted nature', but, in fact, in the mythical world nature as such is supernatural. It is not the nature of the physics of our world. The inner and outer world are not yet understood as separate entities. Let me quote a few examples taken from a well-known book of Maurice Leenhard, *Do Kamo*. When somebody in the mythical world is asked, 'Where is your soul?', he replies that it is to be found in the tree of the ancestors. Man's own entrails are considered as an extension of the vegetation around him. The inner and outer world penetrate each other, and nature has a magic force. A central issue of this type of thinking is *that* something is. The world is a world of fascination, not the universe of contemporary astronomy but the dwelling of divine forces related to society, to the clan, and that world is called socio-mythical space. Man is taken up in the surrounding world. He is in a position of dependence. There is a tendency in our contemporary culture to have a kind of nostalgia for primitive culture. But in a really primitive culture there is not yet any scientific knowledge such as we have. So their world remains different from our world, and we cannot really return to the thinking of the mythical period.

We must add that myth has a demonic element in it. The danger of myth is magic, which is an effort to master reality. This magic force developed by the subject is a danger because it hampers technical and social development. It often produces a life of anxiety, and now and then even a dictatorship of medicine men. This world of myth has no history; it is timeless, it does not develop. What is the subject of this power, this magic force? It is not a being, for the medicine man is only its exponent. The subject is actually the clan itself, not as a sum of individuals but as a magic force: a kind of autonomy of the clan is realized in the magic.

The Period of Ontology

Ontology is that way of thinking which implies a liberation from the fear of magic. The human being is no longer haunted by the supernatural: he is able to put some distance between himself and the surrounding world. He is a subject that is searching for being as being, as Aristotle formulated it. This investigation is a liberation from the magical force of myth, which is mastered by the process of human reflection. This is an evolution, and in it we find the first traces of history, although it is still history against a background of nature. But historical thinking is arising. The divine forces are retiring from nature and daily life to their own supernatural abode. They are no longer dwelling among men as aboriginal forces, but are retiring to Olympus; they are no longer divine forces but are becoming the gods. It is a kind of divinization of the gods and humanization of men. The sacred is separated from the profane, the *templum* from the *agora*, the market place, which in Greece was the particular place of the philosophers. This means that men as well as the gods are taking on a shape of their own. Subject and object in the scheme now stand over against one another as rounded wholes. There is a subject – man – with a soul, and there is an object – nature, the cosmos. Clear divisions of being are now possible, and so science and ontology develop. There is even the natural being and the supernatural being, and thus ontology and metaphysics: ontology describing the structure of the natural being, and metaphysics the supernatural. The central issue of this type of thought is *what* something is, and no longer *that* something is, not the magical force of existing nature but the analysis of what things are. Even the nature of the gods can now be analysed, and there are books written in antiquity under the title of *De Natura Deorum* (*On the Nature of the Gods*). What is a god? That is an interesting subject for a book! The world is no longer a clan or a primitive society, but is gradually becoming a series of kingdoms, gradually arriving at the period of feudalism. There is a kind of political hierarchy in feudalism and also a hierarchy in the realm of being. There is being and higher being, nature and supernature, physics and metaphysics, man and God. And God is the highest being, *Summum Esse*, *Esse Supremum*, *Prima Causa*, etc. There is now a new type of mastery: mastery by reason, reason overwhelming the universe. So reason is becoming 'stand-offish', a substance, a thing existing in itself. Even gods and ethical values are given a status as ontological beings, eternal substances, or essences. This means that the danger of ontological thinking is 'substantialistic' thinking, the isolation of substances, thinking of things in themselves (*Dinge an sich*).

The Period of Functional Thinking

This is the period in which we are at present. Functional thinking is again a liberation from an earlier period, and especially from its dangers. The substances were becoming unreal; they had their own shapes as eternal values – God, the world, etc. – but they were becoming unreal, too far away, too distant. God was too remote, and in particular the word 'God' no longer had any impact on our lives. Now we have a kind of functional thinking, which is not reflection upon isolated substances, but is a kind of tool, a tool of concrete human lives, of the functioning of human society. We can see secularization within this framework. In a secularized world there is no longer an ontological way of thinking, a thinking about higher things, about metaphysical beings. There is no longer a lofty but incomprehensible control of metaphysical entities. In the former period, physics was controlled by metaphysics, by a kind of philosophy. Daily political life was controlled by eternal ethical and moral values. Man in his daily life was under the control of the timeless highest Being, of God. Now we are liberated from all these unreal supernatural entities; they are being eliminated. We ourselves are still in the process of gaining a new freedom. Only that which is directly related to us is real. Things do not exist in themselves; they are no longer substances, but they exist in and for the sake of what they do with us and what we do with them. We are caught up in the power of reality. There is no supernatural reality, high and lofty, above us. There is only that reality which concerns us directly, concretely.

Therefore, according to a functional way of thinking, reality is that which functions, in other words, a thing which becomes a thing to do, an action. The nouns of the ontological era become the verbs of the functional era. Let us take a few examples. What is a religion? Religion in the functional stage is religious behaviour. What are ethical values? In the functional stage they are no longer eternal, supernatural values, a kind of metaphysical control, but ways of organizing and reorganizing societies. As a result of this realization we are enquiring more and more into the meaning of functioning in history. What is the mind? The mind is no longer a thing, a substance, a *res cogitans*, but an action, *cogitare*, the act of thinking. It is no longer an entity in itself. It is not a soul within a subject, but the total historical movement of the human being in social life. To quote a British philosopher, mind is to be observed in the workshop or at the chessboard.

In this functional period subject and object do not stand over against one another as rounded wholes, as they do in the ontological period, but rather they point to one another. They do not exist in themselves but only for each other. This is the natural way of functioning, which is now real. To give another example: what is the meaning of the word 'God'? When you ask this question in the functional stage, in the stage of secularization, you are asking how the word 'God' functions in society. What is the result of the word 'God' in society? Queer, unnatural behaviour in small, religious circles called churches, a kind of behaviour which is interesting perhaps to psychiatrists and cultural anthropologists: is that the meaning of the word 'God'? If the meaning of the word is only *unnatural* behaviour, then the conclusion is that God is unreal.

Let me formulate it another way. In the period of myth, the main issue was *that* something is; in the period of ontological thinking, it was *what* something is; in the period of functional thinking, it is *how* something is, how it functions.

This is reflected in our whole world. It is no longer the world of the clan; it is no longer the world of a series of kingdoms. It is the world of one huge organization. We are all becoming organization-men. We are in a period of industrialization, and men are becoming interdependent. This period is characterized by a new danger which I would call operational thinking. What is the difference between functional thinking and operational thinking? In operational thinking the subject again becomes autonomous. However, the subject is no longer the clan or reason, but organization power, and the object is merely the operation of the subject. I recognize that in some instances this may be the case. The psychologists among you will say that it is the case, for instance, with an I.Q., an Intelligence Quotient. An I.Q. is nothing in itself; it is not a hidden entity in our heads; it is merely the result of certain tests.

But this operational approach can be extended, and here is a very simple example from the philosophical investigations of Ludwig Wittgenstein. It might be called 'the box game'. The rules are as follows. Everybody takes a small box, and then looks for a little beetle to put in it. The beetle may be green or red, or any other colour. You are allowed to look only into your own box. And then you start a discussion about the beetles you have in your boxes. You say, 'Oh, I have a very fine beetle; it is green', and someone replies, 'Oh, mine is very nice; it is yellow'. And so an interesting game develops. This is the game we are always playing in society. You have already recognized yourself in the game. The point of the game is this: you can play the same game when the boxes are empty. And you can play the game with everything – for instance, with religion. We talk to each other about gods. Let us call this game theology. Couldn't we play the same game with empty boxes, when there is no God? The whole thing works very well and you have a very fine theology. This is the extreme consequence, the danger, of operational thinking. The beetle, the I.Q., the soul, God: are they only the result of operation, of certain games?

In modern society also the functional way of life is becoming operational. The importance of an industry is no longer dependent merely upon the number of men it employs, but upon their capacity for organization, their know-how, what I should like to call their 'clean-desk' mentality. A few weeks ago some of my friends visited one of the big bosses of industry. They entered a large building and passed through office after office after office. (Those of you who read Kafka already know the story!) And then they went on, farther and farther, through more and more offices until at last they arrived in the office of the big industrial boss. There he was: no secretary, no tape-recorder, no books, no notes, no papers on his desk. Only a small pencil, a symbol that he was master of the situation. What was he doing there? Why was he the big boss of the industry? He wasn't dictating any letters: he had his personnel to do that. All he was doing was organizing things, and that is important. He was organizing things in new ways, trying to find new combinations. He never does anything 'substantial'. And therein lies the secret of becoming a big industrial boss: never to do anything substantial, because substance belongs to an ontological way of thinking. It is only a question of having 'know-how' and a clean-desk mentality! (Unfortunately I still have many papers on my desk!)

A British report on student life, published by one of the government offices, begins with the following sentence: 'It costs ten thousand pounds to train a student's mind.' This implies that it is not necessary to put a lot of learning into the mind of the student, or to give him higher ethical values, or to bring him into contact with the highest Being, or with eternal values. No, he has only to know how to function, how to operate in society. It costs a lot, but it is worth while. The student is an investment in 'know-how'. It is not a question of his knowing *what* things are, but *how* they are: not of knowing the essence of things, or the substance of things, but how to combine them. We have to become operational, and the danger is that in so doing we shall lose our identity, we shall become nobodies.

A Period of Transition

We are living in a time of very difficult transition from an ontological to a functional way of thinking. Let me now put this in sociological and economic terms. We are living in a period of transition from an agricultural to an industrial society. We in the west often think that we have already an industrial society, that we have had our industrial revolution. But that was just the beginning. I will give only one figure as illustration; you can find others in all reports of the UNO, WHO, UNESCO, etc. At a time when the population of the world is increasing at a fantastic rate, there are in our world five million families working in agriculture. Of these, half a million work with modern equipment – tractors, even radio-guided tractors, and so forth. One and a half million are still tilling the earth with iron ploughs, and the rest – three million families – are still working with wooden ploughs. Most of you have seen wooden ploughs only in museums. Perhaps some of you did not even know that they still exist and are still used. Within twenty-five years these five million families must increase their output by three, four, or five hundred per cent. This means that in a few years they must change from wooden ploughs to iron ploughs, and from iron ploughs to modern equipment. That is not only a technical change, as we so often think: it is a cultural change, a spiritual change. It is a change in outlook, in way of life, involving religion, ethics, and politics. We have to take into account this rapid economic, technical, and historical change. This is the way we live now: we have climbed up to metaphysical reality, and now we are coming down into the daily life of functioning human beings.

The word 'God' can no longer function as a metaphysical entity. It can no longer be used to fill the gaps in our knowledge. There are certain classical quotations you find in every study on secularization. For instance, in the field of physics: when Laplace showed Napoleon his model of the universe, and Napoleon asked him, 'But, Monsieur Laplace, where do you have a place for God?', Laplace answered, 'Sir, I do not need this hypothesis.' In the field of biology, Darwinism substituted the mechanism of evolution for the creative forces of God. In the field of psychology, Freud's psychology of depth described religion as a function of repressed emotion. In the field of sociology, Karl Marx saw it as an ideology for the maintenance of the ruling class. The gaps in our knowledge are now filled up by new discoveries. We are now living in a natural, not a supernatural, world.

So we are coming increasingly to an operational way of living, and I think the danger is obvious enough. Our task is one of renewed liberation. We have first to accept liberation from a remote, metaphysical control: that is the gain of functional thinking. But we have to be careful not to try to replace man by an operation, by 'know-how'. Otherwise our identity is lost and man becomes only an operation of organization power.

Reading the Bible without Metaphysical Presuppositions

And now I come to my concluding remarks. Human thought

always implies the danger of autonomy: the autonomy of magic, of substantialism, or of operationalism. On the other hand, it also implies liberation from repressed hope. Christianity is in danger of becoming supernatural when it remains within the realm of ontological thinking in the sense of metaphysical and substantial thinking. Then religion, and Christianity, become only a metaphysical escape, and others become aware of this before we do ourselves. The biblical message is something quite different from a series of eternal values or sacred traditions or a doctrine of the highest Being. We have to read the Bible without metaphysical or supernatural presuppositions, and this is the meaning of liberation within our era of secularization. It is the advantage of the use of functional thinking in the interpretation of the Bible that we read it without metaphysics, for then the Bible functions directly from human history. The Bible uses myth, but without magic. One example of this is the use of the word 'God' in the Old Testament. It often uses the words 'El' and 'Elohim' which have been taken from paganism. It thus uses a mythical element, but overcomes the inherent danger by giving it a new historical meaning. It uses ontology without substantialism. Another example is the use of the word *pneuma* (spirit) in the New Testament. In stoic theology this word has a substantialistic meaning; but in the New Testament it is used for the unlimited field of God's act, the truth which is not restricted to Jerusalem or Samaria, but is for all men. The Bible also uses functional thinking: it tells a story, a history of hope. The whole story of creation is not a description of nature, as we so often think: it is a description of history.

Let me try to put it yet another way. The word 'God' in the Bible has no meaning as such. But we too often give it a false, supernatural meaning. Then our interpretation stands between us and the Bible itself. In the Bible the word 'God' takes on a meaning. You all know the history of Peniel. The people who lived near the stream of Jabbok thought that in this wild stream, as in every stream, dwelt a godhead, so it was quite natural that one would meet the god when passing the stream by night. And Jacob did meet this god in the night and wrestled with it. This was quite natural, not supernatural. But what was meaningful and made this an historical event was that Jacob did not say, 'Oh, that's the stream god, of course', but rather, 'No, it's He. It's the Name. It is that strange Name which I learned from my father and my grandfather. This must be the God of my father and of my grandfather.' So Jacob said, 'It is the same: it's He again.' Or take the story of the people of Israel passing through the Red Sea. Here again, there is nothing unnatural. The east wind created a passage through the sea, so it was quite natural for the Israelites to say, 'It is the east wind, so we can go through the sea'. And the Egyptians also went through because they said, 'It is the east wind, so we can go through the sea'. But the people of Israel said something more. They said, 'It's He; it is the Name again'. And the result of the story is the historical event: the Egyptians were drowned, but the people of Israel lived. That is history. That is a strange Name acquiring a meaning through the way it functions in history. Or take another example. St Peter often saw the sea. At a certain moment he said, 'Oh, it is the water', just as did the Egyptians, and as the people around Jabbok said, 'Oh, that's the stream god, the natural water'. And so he sank down into the water, because at that moment he did not say, 'It is He again; it is the Name'. He did not recognize the same Name who had been in the Red Sea or at Jabbok. And again, Christ comes and manifests something of that same Name, giving it a new meaning.

The story of the word 'God' is that it has no given meaning, but acquires a meaning in history, as it is presented in the Bible in many ways. There are always people who are saying: 'It is He again; it is the Name.' And then history is made, humanity progresses, and the perspective of hope is revealed. So it is better not to pronounce the Name of God, especially that sacred Name of four letters in the Old Testament which Orthodox Jews never say. The Name is not a doctrine: it is a power overwhelming human reality, but within history, not as a metaphysical control. It is 'God-with-us' (*Immanu-El*). 'God-with-us' is a Name which manifests itself not in a supernatural but in a normal way, as a new meaning of daily events. The visit to Abraham by the

Lord and two angels seems to us like a supernatural event, but it is in fact a quite natural story within the area of myth. In the primitive world of that time a stranger was a godhead. So it was quite natural that the three divine powers should come as strangers. But what was not natural, and what made history, was that Abraham said: 'It is the Name again; it is He who spoke with me.'

So it is in a functional way that man comes into contact with the reality of God, that God acquires a meaning in history. In our own time we look at strangers who come to us and say: 'What you have done to my brethren, you have done to me.' And so I think that in this functional era the Church, as the Church of God, has to speak the same Name as did Jacob, Abraham, and Israel, and has to say again, 'It is the Name'. We have to try to play the game not with empty boxes but in communication with the secularized world of our time. This is a kind of socio-drama, a play in which every participant has to invent spontaneously his role, in response to a given situation, a lecture, or the analysis of a problem. As the Church we have to respond to the world through everything we do; we have to spell out the Name in all our acts. We have to play our game as the World Church, transmitting the old message of a Name – a Name which we do not pronounce too often and too easily: the Name of God, which is taking on a new meaning in history, and especially in the functional history of our time.

5

THEOLOGY AND ANALYTIC PHILOSOPHY

SINCE THE First World War, philosophers in the Anglo-Saxon tradition may fairly be said to have considered that the main (and often the only) task of philosophy is the *analysis* of language – of words, sentences and propositions. They have therefore tended to reject the idea that philosophy is a *synthetic* discipline; that is, that the philosopher through his reason has access to knowledge of reality denied to the sciences, or that his job is to *synthesize* into an over-all, comprehensive, encyclopaedic system the theories and insights garnered by other non-philosophical disciplines.

Analytic philosophy has had a complex history about which it is dangerous to generalize; nevertheless, perhaps we can say this. The early analysts, in their investigations of language, raised very sharply the question of the criteria which distinguished *meaningful* from *meaningless* discourse. In our modern civilization it was perhaps natural that for paradigms of meaningful discourse they should look first and foremost to the language of mathematics and of semi-mathematical empirical sciences like physics. Mathematical language is meaningful in so far as it uses symbols in a correct, consistent way. Thus language which is analogous to mathematics, propositions which correctly utilize symbols and words in a generally agreed way, such as definitions, can without difficulty be regarded as meaningful. But the language of mathematics, or formal logic, or definitions, do not claim to give us information about reality, about the world. That is, they are *non-cognitive*. When we want to investigate language that describes or explains the world (*cognitive* language), it is natural that the language of an empirical science, like physics or chemistry, be considered. What is striking about the language of physical or chemical theories is that it can be boiled down into language describing tests, measurements, observations and predictions which operate to verify or falsify the theories themselves. If such observations and tests were out of the question, it was argued, the language of the theories must be rejected as meaningless. Thus, in the early history of analytic philosophy, 'meaningfulness' was a term which was discussed in the context of mathematics and of the experimental sciences. The language of mathematics and of empirical sciences like physics became normative for meaningful language in general.

How did the language of theology fare within this discussion? Since most theological language did not share the same structure as mathematics or formal logic, it could not be classed as meaningful in the same way as mathematical equations or definitions. But neither did theological language (in so far as it purported to be cognitive, to yield information about the origin, structure and destiny of reality) appear to share the same structure as, say, physics. For it was not apparent that there were empirical tests, measurements or observations that would show theological interpretations to be true or false, as there clearly were in physics. Hence in the nineteen-twenties and in the first half of the 'thirties, when the majority of logical analysts were described as logical positivists, it was common for the language of theology to be rejected as meaningless on the grounds that its assertions were incapable of being shown to be true or false.

Post-war philosophical analysts have been much less rigid and doctrinaire than their pre-war colleagues, and have been willing to concede that meaningful language can be found in many spheres other than those of mathematics or the experimental sciences. This is due partly to the later writings of the Cambridge philosopher Ludwig Wittgenstein (1889-1951), especially his *Philosophical Investigations* (Blackwell, 1953). Hence in the post-war period, philosophers have been willing to look once more at religious language, its nature, structure and possible meaningfulness. If such language is not akin to, say, that of mathematics or chemistry, then what kind of talk is it, what kind of job does it do?

Various answers have been given to these questions, and some of these can be read in the selections in this section. **R. B. Braithwaite,** Knightbridge Professor of Moral Philosophy at Cambridge from 1953 to 1966, in his *An Empiricist's View of the Nature of Religious Belief* (Cambridge UP, 1955), puts forward a non-cognitive view of theological language. Due to its unverifiability or unfalsifiability it cannot function in anything like the same way as a scientific theory, Nevertheless, in Braithwaite's view religious language can perform inestimably valuable services for our lives as men. Braithwaite's views have evoked a considerable world-wide discussion (there is an interesting paper by John Macquarrie in *Studies in Christian Existentialism*, mentioned in section 6 below). Another writer who has put forward a well-known non-cognitive view of religious language and belief is Paul van Buren, in his *The Secular Meaning of the Gospel* (now in Penguin Books). Van Buren also argues that although religious belief does not function at all like a scientific interpretation of the world, the functions it performs may transform and enrich our humanity.

FOR FURTHER READING

William P. Alston, *Philosophy of Language* (Prentice Hall, 1964),

F. Copleston, S.J., *Contemporary Philosophy* (Burns and Oates. 1956).

F. Ferré, *Language, Logic and God* (Fontana Books, 1970).

A. Flew and A. MacIntyre (editors), *New Essays in Philosophical Theology* (SCM Press, 1963).

R. Hepburn, *Christianity and Paradox* (Watts, 1958).

J. Hick, *Philosophy of Religion* (Prentice Hall, 1964).

J. Hick (editor), *The Existence of God* (a book of readings) (Collier-Macmillan, 1964).

J. Macquarrie, *God-Talk* (SCM Press, 1967).

J. A. Martin, *The New Dialogue Between Philosophy and Theology* (A. and C. Black, 1967).

Ian T. Ramsey, *Words about God* (SCM Press, 1971).

J. Urmson, *Philosophical Analysis: Its Development between the Two World Wars* (OUP, 1956).

R. B. Braithwaite · *An Empiricist's View of the Nature of Religious Belief*

The meaning of any statement is given by its method of verification.

The implication of this general principle for the problem of religious belief is that the primary question becomes, not whether a religious statement such as that a personal God created the world is true or is false, but how it could be known either to be true or to be false. Unless this latter question can be answered, the religious statement has no ascertainable meaning and there is nothing expressed by it to be either true or false. Moreover a religious statement cannot be believed without being understood, and it can only be understood by an understanding of the circumstances which would verify or falsify it. Meaning is not logically prior to the possibility of verification: we do not first learn the meaning of a statement, and afterwards consider what would make us call it true or false; the two understandings are one and indivisible.

It would not be correct to say that discussions of religious belief before this present century have always ignored the problem of meaning, but until recently the emphasis has been upon the question of the truth or the reasonableness of religious beliefs rather than upon the logically prior question as to the meaning of the statements expressing the beliefs. The argument usually proceeded as if we all knew what was meant by the statement that a personal God created the world; the point at issue was whether or not this statement was true, or whether there were good reasons for believing it. But if the meaning of a religious statement has to be found by discovering the steps which must be taken to ascertain its truth-value, an examination of the methods for testing the statement for truth-value is an essential preliminary to any discussion as to which of the truth-values – truth or falsity – holds of the statement.

There are three classes of statement whose method of truth-value testing is in general outline clear: statements about particular matters of empirical fact, scientific hypotheses and other general empirical statements, and the logically necessary statements of logic and mathematics (and their contradictories). Do religious statements fall into any of these three classes? If they do, the problem of their meaningfulness will be solved: their truth-values will be testable by the methods appropriate to empirical statements, particular or general, or to mathematical statements. It seems to me clear that religious statements, as they are normally used, have no place in this trichotomy. I shall give my reasons very briefly, since I have little to add here to what other empiricist philosophers have said.

I. Statements about particular empirical facts are testable by direct observation. The only facts that can be directly known by observation are that the things observed have certain observable properties or stand in certain observable relations to one another. If it is maintained that the *existence* of God is known by observation, for example, in the 'self-authenticating' experience of 'meeting God', the term 'God' is being used merely as part of the description of that particular experience. Any interesting theological proposition, e.g. that God is personal, will attribute a property to God which is not an observable one and so cannot be known by direct observation. Comparison with our knowledge of other people is an unreal comparison. I can get to know things about an intimate friend at a glance, but this knowledge is not self-authenticating; it is based upon a great deal of previous knowledge about the connection between facial and bodily expressions and states of mind.

II. The view that would class religious statements with scientific hypotheses must be taken much more seriously. It would be very unplausible if a Baconian methodology of science had to be employed, and scientific hypotheses taken as simple generalizations from particular instances, for then there could be no understanding of a general theological proposition unless particular instances of it could be directly observed. But an advanced science has progressed far beyond its natural history stage; it makes use in its explanatory hypotheses of concepts of a high degree of abstractness and at a far remove from experience. These theoretical concepts are given a meaning by the place they occupy in a deductive system consisting of hypotheses of different degrees of generality in which the least general hypotheses, deducible from the more general ones, are generalizations of observable facts. So it is no valid criticism of the view that would treat God as an empirical concept entering into an explanatory hypothesis to say that God is not directly observable. No more is an electric field of force or a Schrödinger wave-function. There is no *prima facie* objection to regarding such a proposition as that there is a God who created and sustains the world as an explanatory scientific hypothesis.

But if a set of theological propositions are to be regarded as scientific explanations of facts in the empirical world, they must be refutable by experience. We must be willing to abandon them if the facts prove different from what we think they are. A hypothesis which is consistent with every possible empirical fact is not an empirical one. And though the theoretical concepts in a hypothesis need not be explicity definable in terms of direct observation – indeed they must not be if the system is to be applicable to novel situations – yet they must be related to some and not to all of the possible facts in the world in order to have a non-vacuous significance. If there is a personal God, how would the world be different if there were not? Unless this question can be answered God's existence cannot be given an empirical meaning.

At earlier times in the history of religion God's personal existence has been treated as a scientific hypothesis subjectable to empirical test. Elijah's contest with the prophets of Baal was an experiment to test the hypothesis that Jehovah and not Baal controlled the physical world. But most educated believers at the present time do not think of God as being detectable in this sort of way, and hence do not think of theological propositions as explanations of facts in the world of nature in the way in which established scientific hypotheses are.

It may be maintained, however, that theological propositions explain facts about the world in another way. Not perhaps the physical world, for physical science has been so successful with its own explanations; but the facts of biological and psychological development. Now it is certainly the case that a great deal of traditional Christian language – phrases such as 'original sin', 'the old Adam', 'the new man', 'growth in holiness' – can be given meanings within statements expressing general hypotheses about human personality. Indeed it is hardly too much to say that almost all statements about God as immanent, as an indwelling spirit, can be interpreted as asserting psychological facts in metaphorical language. But would those interpreting religious statements in this way be prepared to abandon them if the empirical facts were found to be different? Or would they rather re-interpret them to fit the new facts? In the latter case the possibility of interpreting them to fit experience is not enough to give an empirical meaning to the statements. Mere consistency with experience without the possibility of inconsistency does not determine meaning. And a metaphorical description is not in itself an explanation. This criticism also holds against attempts to interpret theism as an explanation of the course of history, unless it is admitted (which few theists would be willing to admit) that, had the course of history been different in some specific way, God would not have existed.

Philosophers of religion who wish to make empirical facts relevant to the meaning of religious statements but at the same time desire to hold on to these statements whatever the empirical facts may be are indulging, I believe, in a sort of 'double-think' attitude: they want to hold that religious statements both are about the actual world (i.e. are empirical statements) and also are not refutable in any possible world, the characteristic of statements which are logically necessary.

III. The view that statements of natural theology resemble the propositions of logic and mathematics in being logically necessary would have as a consequence that they make no assertion of existence. Whatever exactly be the status of logically necessary propositions, Hume and Kant have conclusively shown that they are essentially hypothetical. $2+3 = 5$ makes no assertion about there being any things in the world; what it says is that, *if* there is a class of five things in the world, *then* this class is the union of two mutually exclusive sub-classes, one comprising two and the other comprising three things. The logical-positivist thesis, due to Wittgenstein, that the truth of this hypothetical proposition is verified not by any logical fact about the world but by the way in which we use numerical symbols in our thinking goes further than Kant did in displacing logic and mathematics from the world of reality. But it is not necessary to accept this more radical thesis in order to agree with Kant that no logically necessary proposition can assert existence; and this excludes the possibility of regarding theological propositions as logically necessary in the way in which the hypothetical propositions of mathematics and logic are necessary.

The traditional arguments for a Necessary God – the ontological and the cosmological – were elaborated by Anselm and the scholastic philosophers before the concurrent and interrelated development of natural science and of mathematics had enabled necessity and contingency to be clearly distinguished. The necessity attributed by these arguments to the being of God may perhaps be different from the logical necessity of mathematical truths; but, if so, no method has been provided for testing the truth-value of the statement that God is necessary being, and consequently no way given for assigning meaning to the terms 'necessary being' and 'God'.

If religious statements cannot be held to fall into any of these three classes, their method of verification cannot be any of the standard methods applicable to statements falling in these classes. Does this imply that religious statements are not verifiable, with the corollary, according to the verificational principle, that they have no meaning and, though they purport to say something, are in fact nonsensical sentences? The earlier logical positivists thought so: they would have echoed the demand of their precursor Hume that a volume ('of divinity or school metaphysics') which contains neither 'any abstract reasoning concerning quantity or number' nor 'any experimental reasoning concerning matter of fact and existence' should be committed to the flames; though their justification for the holocaust would be even more cogent than Hume's. The volume would not contain even 'sophistry and illusion': it would contain nothing but meaningless marks of printer's ink.

Religious statements, however, are not the only statements which are unverifiable by standard methods; moral statements have the same peculiarity. A moral principle, like the utilitarian principle that a man ought to act so as to maximize happiness, does not seem to be either a logically necessary or a logically impossible proposition. But neither does it seem to be an empirical proposition, all the attempts of ethical empiricists to give naturalistic analyses having failed. Though a tough-minded logical positivist might be prepared to say that all religious statements are sound and fury, signifying nothing, he can hardly say that of all moral statements. For moral statements have a use in guiding conduct; and if they have a use they surely have a meaning – in some sense of meaning. So the verificational principle of meaning in the hands of empiricist philosophers in the 1930s became modified either by a glossing of the term 'verification' or by a change of the verification principle into the use principle: the meaning of any statement is given by the way in which it is used.

Since I wish to continue to employ verification in the restricted sense of ascertaining truth-value, I shall take the principle of meaning in this new form in which the word 'verification' has disappeared. But in removing this term from the statement of the principle, there is no desertion from the spirit of empiricism. The older verificational principle is subsumed under the new use principle: the use of an empirical statement derives from the fact that the statement is empirically verifiable, and the logical-positivist thesis of the 'linguistic' character of logical and mathematical statements can be equally well, if not better, expressed in terms of their use than of their method of verification. Moreover the only way of discovering how a statement need not itself be empirically verifiable, but that it is used in a particular way, is always a straightforwardly empirical proposition.

The meaning of any statement, then, will be taken as being given by the way it is used. The kernel for an empiricist of the problem of the nature of religious belief is to explain, in empirical terms, how a religious statement is used by a man who asserts it in order to express his religious conviction. . . .

The way to find out what are the intentions embodied in a set of religious assertions, and hence what is the meaning of the assertions, is by discovering what principles of conduct the asserter takes the assertions to involve. These may be ascertained both by asking him questions and by seeing how he behaves, each test being supplemental to the other. If what is wanted is not the meaning of the religious assertions made by a particular man, but what the set of assertions would mean were they to be made by anyone of the same religion (which I will call their *typical* meaning), all that can be done is to specify the form of behaviour which is in accordance with what one takes to be the fundamental moral principles of the religion in question. Since different people will take different views as to what these fundamental principles are, the typical meaning of religious assertions will be different for different people. I myself take the typical meaning of the body of Christian assertions as being given by their proclaiming intentions to follow an agapeistic way of life, and for a description of this way of life – a description in general and metaphorical terms, but an empirical description nevertheless – I should quote most of the thirteenth chapter of I Corinthians. Others may think that the Christian way of life should be described somewhat differently, and will therefore take the typical meaning of the assertions of Christianity to correspond to their different view of its fundamental moral teaching.

My contention, then, is that the primary use of religious assertions is to announce allegiance to a set of moral principles: without such allegiance there is no 'true religion'. This is borne out by all the accounts of what happens when an unbeliever becomes converted to a religion. The conversion is not only a change in the propositions believed – indeed there may be no specifically intellectual change at all; it is a change in the state of will. An excellent instance is C. S. Lewis's recently published account of his conversion from an idealist metaphysic – 'a religion (as he says) that cost nothing' – to a theism where he faced (and he quotes George Macdonald's phrase) 'something to be neither more nor less nor other than *done*'. There was no intellectual change, for (as he says) 'there had long been an ethic (theoretically) attached to my Idealism': it was the recognition that he had to do something about it, that 'an attempt at complete virtue must be made'. His conversion was a re-orientation of the will.

In assimilating religious assertions to moral assertions I do not wish to deny that there are any important differences. One is the fact already noticed that usually the behaviour policy intended is not specified by one religious assertion in isolation. Another difference is that the fundamental moral teaching of the religion is frequently given, not in abstract terms, but by means of concrete examples – of how to behave, for instance, if one meets a man set upon by thieves on the road to Jericho. A resolution to behave like the good Samaritan does not, in itself, specify the behaviour to be resolved upon in quite different circumstances. However, absence of explicitly recognized general principles does not prevent a man from acting in accordance with such principles; it only makes it more difficult for a questioner to discover upon what principles he is acting. And the difficulty is not only one way round. If moral principles are stated in the most general form, as most moral philosophers have wished to state them, they tend to become so far removed from particular courses of conduct that it is difficult, if not impossible, to give them any precise content. It may be hard to find out what exactly is in-involved in the imitation of Christ; but it is not very easy to discover what exactly is meant by the pursuit of Aristotle's *eudaemonia* or of Mill's *happiness*. The tests for what it is to live agapeistically are as empirical as are those for living in quest of happiness; but in each case the tests can best be expounded in terms of examples of particular situations.

A more important difference between religious and purely moral principles is that, in the higher religions at least, the conduct preached by the religion concerns not only external but also internal behaviour. The conversion involved in accepting a religion is a conversion not only of the will but of the heart. Christianity requires not only that you should behave towards your neighbour as if you loved him as yourself: it requires that you should love him as yourself. And though I have no doubt that the Christian concept of *agape* refers partly to external behaviour – the agapeistic behaviour for which there are external criteria – yet being filled with *agape* includes more than behaving agapeistically externally: it also includes an agapeistic frame of mind. I have said that I cannot regard the expression of a feeling of any sort as the primary element in religious assertion; but this does not imply that intention to feel in a certain way is not a primary element, nor that it cannot be used to discriminate religious declarations of policy from declarations which are merely moral. Those who say that Confucianism is a code of morals and not, properly speaking, a religion are, I think, making this discrimination.

The resolution proclaimed by a religious assertion may then be taken as referring to inner life as well as to outward conduct. And the superiority of religious conviction over the mere adoption of a moral code in securing conformity to the code arises from a religious conviction changing what the religious man wants. It may be hard enough to love your enemy, but once you have succeeded in doing so it is easy to behave lovingly towards him. But if you continue to hate him, it requires a heroic perseverance continually to behave as if you loved him. Resolutions to feel, even if they are only partly fulfilled, are powerful reinforcements of resolutions to act.

But though these qualifications may be adequate for distinguishing religious assertions from purely moral ones, they are not sufficient to discriminate between assertions belonging to one religious system and those belonging to another system in the case in which the behaviour policies, both of inner life and of outward conduct, inculcated by the systems are identical. For instance, I have said that I take the fundamental moral teaching of Christianity to be the preaching of an agapeistic way of life. But a Jew or a Buddhist may, with considerable plausibility, maintain that the fundamental moral teaching of his religion is to recommend exactly the same way of life. How then can religious assertions be distinguished into those which are Christian, those which are Jewish, those which are Buddhist, by the policies of life which they respectively recommend if, on examination, these policies turn out to be the same?

Many Christians will, no doubt, behave in a specifically Christian manner in that they will follow ritual practices which are Christian and neither Jewish nor Buddhist. But though following certain practices may well be the proper test for membership of a particular religious society, a church, not even the most ecclesiastically-minded Christian will regard participation in a ritual as the fundamental characteristic of a Christian way of life. There must be some more important difference between an agapeistically policied Christian and an agapeistically policied Jew than that the former attends a church and the latter a synagogue.

The really important difference, I think, is to be found in the fact that the intentions to pursue the behaviour policies, which may be the same for different religions, are associated with thinking of different *stories* (or sets of stories). By a story I shall here mean a proposition or set of propositions which are straightforwardly empirical propositions capable of empirical test and which are thought of by the religious man in connection with his resolution to follow the way of life advocated by his religion. On the assumption that the ways of life advocated by Christianity and by Buddhism are essentially the same, it will be the fact that the intention to follow this way of life is associated in the mind of a Christian with thinking of one set of stories (the Christian stories) while it is associated in the mind of a Buddhist with thinking of another set of stories (the Buddhist stories) which enables a Christian assertion to be distinguished from a Buddhist one.

A religious assertion will, therefore, have a propositional element which is lacking in a purely moral assertion, in that it will refer to a story as well as to an intention. The reference to the story is not an assertion of the story taken as a matter of empirical fact: it is a telling of the story, or an alluding to the story, in the way in which one can tell, or allude to, the story of a novel with which one is acquainted. To assert the whole set of assertions of the Christian religion is both to tell the Christian doctrinal story and to confess allegiance to the Christian way of life.

The story, I have said, is a set of empirical propositions, and the language expressing the story is given a meaning by the standard method of understanding how the story-statements can be verified. The empirical story-statements will vary from Christian to Christian; the doctrines of Christianity are capable of different empirical interpretations, and Christians will differ in the interpretations they put upon the doctrines. But the interpretations will all be in terms of empirical propositions. Take, for example, the doctrine of Justification by means of the Atonement. Matthew Arnold imagined it in terms of

> . . . a sort of infinitely magnified and improved Lord Shaftesbury, with a race of vile offenders to deal with, whom his natural goodness would incline him to let off, only his sense of justice will not allow it; then a younger Lord Shaftesbury, on the scale of his father and very dear to him, who might live in grandeur and splendour if he liked, but who prefers to leave his home, to go and live among the race of offenders, and to be put to an ignominious death, on condition that his merits shall be counted against their demerits, and that his father's goodness shall be restrained no longer from taking effect, but any offender shall be admitted to the benefit of it on simply pleading the satisfaction made by the son; – and then, finally, a third Lord Shaftesbury, still on the same high scale, who keeps very much in the background, and works in a very occult manner, but very efficaciously nevertheless, and who is busy in applying everywhere the benefits of the son's satisfaction and the father's goodness.

Arnold's 'parable of the three Lord Shaftesburys' got him into a lot of trouble: he was 'indignantly censured' (as he says) for wounding 'the feelings of the religious community by turning into ridicule an august doctrine, the object of their solemn faith'. But there is no other account of the Anselmian doctrine of the Atonement that I have read which puts it in so morally favourable a light. Be that as it may, the only way in which the doctrine can be understood verificationally is in terms of human beings – mythological beings, it may be, who never existed, but who nevertheless would have been empirically observable had they existed.

For it is not necessary, on my view, for the asserter of a religious assertion to believe in the truth of the story involved in the assertions: what is necessary is that the story should be entertained in thought, i.e. that the statement of the story should be understood as having a meaning. I have secured this by requiring that the story should consist of empirical propositions. Educated Christians of the present day who attach importance to the doctrine of the Atonement certainly do not believe an empirically testable story in Matthew Arnold's or any other form. But it is the fact that entertainment in thought of this and other Christian stories forms the context in which Christian resolutions are made which serves to distinguish Christian assertions from those made by adherents of another religion, or of no religion.

What I am calling a story Matthew Arnold called a *parable* and a *fairy-tale*. Other terms which might be used are *allegory*, *fable*, *tale*, *myth*. I have chosen the word 'story' as being the most neutral term, implying neither that the story is believed nor that it is disbelieved. The Christian stories include straightforward historical statements about the life and death of Jesus of Nazareth; a Christian (unless he accepts the unplausible Christ-myth theory) will naturally believe some or all of these. Stories about the beginning of the world and of the Last Judgment as facts of past or of future history are believed by many unsophisticated Christians. But my contention is that belief in the truth of the Christian stories is not the proper criterion for deciding whether or not an assertion is a Christian one. A man is not, I think, a professing Christian unless he both proposes to live according to Christian moral principles and associates his intention with thinking of Christian stories; but he need not believe that the empirical propositions presented by the stories correspond to empirical fact.

But if the religious stories need not be believed, what function do they fulfil in the complex state of mind and behaviour known as having a religious belief? How is entertaining the story related to resolving to pursue a certain way of life? My answer is that the relation is a psychological and casual one. It is an empirical psychological fact that many people find it easier to resolve upon and to carry through a course of action which is contrary to their natural inclinations if this policy is associated in their minds with certain stories. And in many people the psychological link is not appreciably weakened by the fact that the story associated with the behaviour policy is not believed. Next to the Bible and the Prayer Book the most influential work in English Christian religious life has been a book whose stories are frankly recognized as fictitious – Bunyan's *Pilgrim's Progress*; and some of the most influential works in setting the moral tone of my generation were the novels of Dostoievsky. It is completely untrue, as a matter of psychological fact, to think that the only intellectual considerations which affect action are beliefs: it is *all* the thoughts of a man that determine his behaviour; and these include his phantasies, imaginations, ideas of what he would wish to be and do, as well as the propositions which he believes to be true. . . .

There is one story common to all the moral theistic religions which has proved of great psychological value in enabling religious men to persevere in carrying out their religious behaviour policies – the story that in so doing they are doing the will of God. And here it may look as if there is an intrinsic connection between the story and the policy of conduct. But even when the story is literally believed, when it is believed that there is a magnified Lord Shaftesbury who commands or desires the carrying out of the behaviour policy, that in itself is no reason for carrying out the policy: it is necessary also to have the intention of doing what the magnified Lord Shaftesbury commands or desires. But the intention to do what a person commands or desires, irrespective of what this command or desire may be, is no part of a higher religion; it is when the religious man finds that what the magnified Lord Shaftesbury commands or desires accords with his own moral judgment that he decides to obey or to accede to it. But this is no new decision, for his own moral judgment is a decision to carry out a behaviour policy; all that is happening is that he is describing his old decision in a new way. In religious conviction the resolution to follow a way of life is primary; it is not derived from believing, still less from thinking of, any empirical story.

The story may psychologically support the resolution, but it does not logically justify it.

In this lecture I have been sparing in my use of the term 'religious belief' (although it occurs in the title), preferring instead to speak of religious assertions and of religious conviction. This was because for me the fundamental problem is that of the meaning of statements used to make religious assertions, and I have accordingly taken my task to be that of explaining the use of such assertions, in accordance with the principle that meaning is to be found by ascertaining use. In disentangling the elements of this use I have discovered nothing which can be called 'belief' in the senses of this word applicable either to an empirical or to a logically necessary proposition. A religious assertion, for me, is the assertion of an intention to carry out a certain behaviour policy, subsumable under a sufficiently general principle to be a moral one, together with the implicit or explicit statement, but not the assertion, of certain stories. Neither the assertion of the intention nor the reference to the stories includes belief in its ordinary senses. But in avoiding the term 'belief' I have had to widen the term 'assertion', since I do not pretend that either the behaviour policy intended or the stories entertained are adequately specified by the sentences used in making isolated religious assertions. So assertion has been extended to include elements not explicitly expressed in the verbal form of the assertion. If we drop the linguistic expression of the assertion altogether the remainder is what may be called religious belief. Like moral belief, it is not a species of ordinary belief, of belief in a proposition. A moral belief is an intention to behave in a certain way: a religious belief is an intention to behave in a certain way (a moral belief) together with the entertainment of certain stories associated with the intention in the mind of the believer. This solution of the problem of religious belief seems to me to do justice both to the empiricist's demand that meaning must be tied to empirical use and to the religious man's claim for his religious beliefs to be taken seriously.

Seriously, it will be retorted, but not objectively. If a man's religion is all a matter of following the way of life he sets before himself and of strengthening his determination to follow it by imagining exemplary fairy-tales, it is purely subjective: his religion is all in terms of his own private ideals and of his own private imaginations. How can he even try to convert others to his religion if there is nothing objective to convert them to? How can he argue in its defence if there is no religious proposition which he believes, nothing which he takes to be the fundamental truth about the universe? And is it of any public interest what mental techniques he uses to bolster up his will? Discussion about religion must be more than the exchange of autobiographies.

But we are all social animals; we are all members one of another. What is profitable to one man in helping him to persevere in the way of life he has decided upon may well be profitable to another man who is trying to follow a similar way of life; and to pass on information that might prove useful would be approved by almost every morality. The autobiography of one man may well have an influence upon the life of another, if their basic wants are similar.

But suppose that these are dissimilar, and that the two men propose to conduct their lives on quite different fundamental principles. Can there be any reasonable discussion between them? This is the problem that has faced the many moral philosophers recently who have been forced, by their examination of the nature of thinking, into holding non-propositional theories of ethics. All I will here say is that to hold that the adoption of a set of moral principles is a matter of personal decision to live according to these principles does not imply that beliefs as to what are the practical consequences of following such principles are not relevant to the decision. An intention, it is true, cannot be logically based upon anything except another intention. But in considering what conduct to intend to practise, it is highly relevant whether or not the consequences of practising that conduct are such as one would intend to secure. As R. M. Hare has well said, an ultimate decision to accept a way of life, 'far from being arbitrary, . . . would be the most well-founded of decisions, because it would be based upon a consideration of everything upon which it could possibly be founded.' And in this consideration there is a place for every kind of rational argument.

Whatever may be the case with other religions Christianity has always been a personal religion demanding personal commitment to a personal way of life. In the words of another Oxford philosopher, 'the questions "What shall I do?" and "What moral principles should I adopt?" must be answered by each man for himself.' Nowell-Smith takes this as part of the meaning of morality: whether or not this is so, I am certain that it is of the very essence of the Christian religion.

The three parables in this section were composed by the Cambridge philosopher **John Wisdom,** the Oxford philosopher **Basil Mitchell,** and the Cambridge philosopher of religion **John Hick**. The main points made by these three parables seem to be these. All three point to the ambiguity of the world and of our experience in it. When the Christian expounds and defends his belief he is describing an over-all pattern which he claims to find in it. On the other hand, when the agnostic explains his inability to accept religious beliefs he is really pointing to those disjointed and tragic elements in experience which prevent him from involving himself in a quest to vindicate any over-all pattern which might give meaning to the whole. Mitchell and Hick are both Christians while Wisdom is not, and this fact is reflected in the differences we can detect in the parables they offer. The characters in the stories of the first two *commit* themselves in a practical way to the pattern which they claim to detect in the whole. Their commitment alters their way of life. This points to the Christian emphasis on faith, commitment, involvement and trust, attitudes which involve grave consequences for the development of human personalities. Again, the parables of the two Christians point towards the possibility of a future vindication of whether the trust and commitment were justified or not. Indeed, Hick has expounded the theory that the Christian interpretation of experience can in principle be verified after human life in the world has come to an end, at the Last Things, a theory which Hick has labelled 'a theory of eschatological verification' (see his *Philosophy of Religion*). What is also striking about these parables (and very typical of contemporary philosophical theology) is that when the parties disagree about the over-all meaning of human experience, neither party can bludgeon the other by, say, coercive arguments, into accepting one view rather than the other. The ambiguity of the world and of experience cannot be dissolved away in this manner. The world remains a place where free decision and commitment are demanded, but the decision is such that it affects human nature and destiny in a uniquely significant way. A commentary on the three parables, and a theological approach which makes constructive use of the insights contained in them, is to be found in James Richmond, *Theology and Metaphysics* (SCM Press, 1970).

John Wisdom · *The Garden*

Two people return to their long neglected garden and find among the weeds a few of the old plants surprisingly vigorous. One says to the other, 'It must be that a gardener has been coming and doing something about these plants.' Upon inquiry they find that no neighbour has ever seen anyone at work in their garden. The first man says to the other, 'He must have worked while people slept.' The other says, 'No, someone would have heard him and besides, anybody who cared about the plants would have kept down these weeds.' The first man says, 'Look at the way these are arranged. There is purpose and a feeling for beauty here. I believe that someone comes, someone invisible to mortal eyes. I believe that the more carefully we look the more we shall find confirmation of this.' They examine the garden ever so carefully and sometimes they come on new things suggesting that a gardener comes and sometimes they come on new things suggesting the contrary and even that a malicious person has been at work. Besides examining the garden carefully they also study what happens to gardens left without attention. Each learns all the other learns about this and about the garden. Consequently, when after all this one says, 'I still believe a gardener comes', while the other says 'I don't', their different words now reflect no difference as to what they have found in the garden, no difference as to what they would find in the garden if they looked further and no difference about how fast untended gardens fall into disorder. At this stage, in this context, the gardener hypothesis has ceased to be experimental, the difference between one who accepts and one who rejects it is now not a matter of the one expecting something the other does not expect. What is the difference between them? The one says 'A gardener comes unseen and unheard. He is manifested only in his works with which we are all familiar'; the other says 'There is no gardener', and with this difference in what they say about the gardener goes a difference in how they feel towards the garden, in spite of the fact that neither expects anything of it which the other does not expect.

But is this the whole difference between them – that the one calls the garden by one name and feels one way towards it, while the other calls it by another name and feels in another way towards it? And if this is what the difference has become then is it any longer appropriate to ask 'Which is right?' or 'Which is reasonable?'?

And yet surely such questions are appropriate when one person says to another 'You still think the world's a garden and not a wilderness, and that the gardener has not forsaken it' or 'You still think there are nymphs of the streams, a presence in the hills, a spirit of the world'. Perhaps when a man sings 'God's in his heaven' we need not take this as more than an expression of how he feels. But when Bishop Gore or Dr Joad write about belief in God and young men read them in order to settle their religious doubts the impression is not simply that of persons choosing exclamations with which to face nature and the 'changes and chances of this mortal life'. The disputants speak as if they are concerned with a matter of scientific fact, or of trans-sensual, trans-scientific and metaphysical fact, but still of fact and still a matter about which reasons for and against may be offered, although no scientific reasons in the sense of field surveys for fossils or experiments on delinquents are to the point.

Basil Mitchell · *The Stranger*

In time of war in an occupied country, a member of the resistance meets one night a stranger who deeply inpresses him. They spend that night together in conversation. The Stranger tells the partisan that he himself is on the side of the resistance – indeed that he is in command of it, and urges the partisan to have faith in him no matter what happens. The partisan is utterly convinced at that meeting of the Stranger's sincerity and constancy and undertakes to trust him.

They never meet in conditions of intimacy again. But sometimes the Stranger is seen helping members of the resistance, and the partisan is grateful and says to his friends, 'He is on our side'.

Sometimes he is seen in the uniform of the police handing over patriots to the occupying power. On these occasions his friends murmur against him: but the partisan still says, 'He is on our side'. He still believes that, in spite of appearances, the Stranger did not deceive him. Sometimes he asks the Stranger for help and receives it. He is then thankful. Sometimes he asks and does not receive it. Then he says, 'The Stranger knows best'. Sometimes his friends, in exasperation, say, 'Well, what would he have to do for you to admit that you were wrong and that he is not on our side?' But the partisan refuses to answer. He will not consent to put the Stranger to the test. And sometimes his friends complain: 'Well, if that's what you mean by his being on our side, the sooner he goes over to the other side the better.'

The partisan of the parable does not allow anything to count decisively against the proposition 'The Stranger is on our side'. This is because he has committed himself to trust the Stranger. But he of course recognizes that the Stranger's ambiguous behaviour does count against what he believes about him. It is precisely this situation which constitutes the trial of his faith.

John Hick · *The Road*

Two men are travelling together along a road. One of them believes that it leads to the Celestial City, the other that it leads nowhere; but since this is the only road there is, both must travel it. Neither has been this way before; therefore, neither is able to say what they will find around each corner. During their journey they meet with moments of refreshment and delight, and with moments of hardship and danger. All the time one of them thinks of his journey as a pilgrimage to the Celestial City. He interprets the pleasant parts as encouragements and the obstacles as trials of his purpose and lessons in endurance, prepared by the king of that city and designed to make of him a worthy citizen of the place when at last he arrives. The other, however, believes none of this, and sees their journey as an unavoidable and aimless ramble. Since he has no choice in the matter, he enjoys the good and endures the bad. For him there is no Celestial City to be reached, no all-encompassing purpose ordaining their journey; there is only the road itself and the luck of the road in good weather and in bad.

During the course of the journey, the issue between them is not an experimental one. They do not entertain different expectations about the coming details of the road, but only about its ultimate destination. Yet, when they turn the last corner, it will be apparent that one of them has been right all the time and the other wrong. Thus, although the issue between them has not been experimental; it has, nevertheless, been a real issue. They have not merely felt differently about the road, for one was feeling appropriately and the other inappropriately in relation to the actual state of affairs. Their opposed interpretations of the situation have constituted genuinely rival assertions, whose assertion-status has the peculiar characteristic of being guaranteed retrospectively by a future crux.

This parable, like all parables, has narrow limitations. It is designed to make only one point: that Judaic-Christian theism postulates an ultimate unambiguous existence *in patria*, as well as our present ambiguous existence *in via*. There is a state of having arrived as well as a state of journeying, an eternal heavenly life as well as an earthly pilgrimage. The alleged future experience cannot, of course, be appealed to as evidence for theism as a present interpretation of our experience; but it does suffice to render the choice between theism and atheism a real and not merely an empty or verbal choice.

6

COMMENTS AND REACTIONS

THE PRECEDING sections have raised a number of problems for theology and have left a great many questions unanswered. In which direction is a way forward to be found? These last three passages, all by British theologians, comment on the difficulties and offer positive suggestions for further progress. While the writers are conscious of the pressures on contemporary theology, they are agreed that the future prospect is by no means a gloomy one.

H. D. Lewis, Head of the Department of the History and Philosophy of Religion in the University of London, accepts the challenge of empiricist philosophy and linguistic analysis and allows the validity of many of its criticisms. Unlike, for example, Paul van Buren in his *The Secular Meaning of the Gospel* (now in Penguin Books), he is unwilling to accept all the terms which it dictates, and indicates clearly where its limits lie. Additional comments, and a very wide selection of material for further reading, are to be found in his *Philosophy of Religion* (English Universities Press, 1965), from which this extract is taken.

H. D. Lewis · *The Limits and Lessons of Empiricism*

We have been concerned with attempts to come to terms with empiricism and the positions associated with it in contemporary thought. There are many, however, who believe that this is not the proper course to take. They think that empiricism can be refuted and that this opens the way for a less tortuous defence of religion and the affirmation of its claims afresh in senses not so radically different from their normal and traditional meaning as the compromises which we have just been noting. The refutation of empiricism takes two main forms. One is to bring out internal strains and inconsistencies in the presentation of the empiricist position. These appear especially when claims of a general or universal nature are made, for example the insistence that *all* knowledge must be derived from sense experience or based on observation. How do we know that these conditions *must* apply to *all* knowledge? Is there an empiricist way of establishing this principle itself? Can the 'principle of verification' be verified? Attempts are made to counter this by describing the principle of verification or some other less rigid form of empiricism as statements of a rule or method of procedure or as a convention which does not itself claim truth. But this is a difficult position to justify without opening the door to many things which the empiricist does not usually want to admit. Nor does it seem to me very plausible in itself as a defence of a philosophical view. The second way of meeting the challenge of empiricism is a more direct one. It consists in noting features of our thought or experience of which it is extremely difficult to give an exhaustive account in empiricist terms. Of these the following are outstanding examples.

Firstly there are the principles of logic itself, including the law of contradiction. We take it to be absurd of us to contradict ourselves, and a common feature of all controversy is the attempt to show that one's opponent is not consistent. No one wants to plead guilty to out-and-out inconsistency. We may find a use for suggestive paradox, we may affirm things which seem inconsistent, or are verbally so, without being inconsistent in fact. But how do we know that we must not contradict ourselves, that it is absurd to suppose that I am in this room now and, in the same sense, elsewhere? There seems to be no answer to this question. We just see the absurdity involved. We do not derive it from some kind of experience. We must of course have some experience to know when we are contradicting ourselves, and we shall also have the unpleasant experience of finding ourselves in much practical difficulty if we set consistency at naught. But these are not reasons which convince us that it is absurd to contradict ourselves. I know without further ado that I cannot be in this room and playing on the lawn, except in some unusual and metaphorical use of one or the other of these terms, as when I may be said to be 'in thought' playing tennis outside. The principle of contradiction is, in technical language, *a priori*, that is the validation of it does not depend directly on experience. But this principle is basic to all our thinking and there seems thus to be something non-empirical at the centre of all thought and experience.

We may take a similar line about further truths of logic and about mathematics. We do not know that twice two are four because that is how it has always turned out in our experience. We know that the answer *must* be four and that this is true of every situation or world of which we can think. It just cannot be otherwise. We could, of course, in a quibble, say that two rabbits, in breeding, produce many more, but this biological fact has nothing to do with multiplication in the strict mathematical sense. Likewise we prove that the sum of the angles of a triangle is 180 degrees without thinking at all of sampling various triangles to see whether this is true. We know something in these cases in some way which is quite different from the knowledge we have that flames are hot. We can conceive of flames being cold; this might be difficult but the idea is not at any rate self-contradictory. We know that two and two just could not be five. Sampling is unnecessary and irrelevant here, and as soon as we have understood the matter we know that the angles of a triangle *must* be 180 degrees.

In reply to this, it is sometimes maintained that these principles of logic and mathematics do not claim truth in the proper sense, they are definitions, tautologies, rules of procedure, and so on. As such they are also variable. There can be 'alternative logics' and 'alternative geometries'. This seems to me very hard to sustain. That twice two are four seems so evident the moment we understand what is meant that it might seem plausible to regard it as a tautology, that is as containing no new information. But this is much less plausible when we turn to more complicated calculations in arithmetic or geometry. We know what 245 and 367 mean without having any notion what they will yield when multiplied. That would take time to discover, and the solutions to some problems require exceptional gifts, and in some cases genius, to discover them. Surely we learn something new in the process. As for the notion of alternative geometries and logics, I believe these will be found, on proper inspection, to involve alternative systems which do not in fact come to the same thing at all, that is they do not really contradict one another or provide strict alternatives. This would take long to debate, it is one of the central matters in controversy today in philosophy, and the reader should try to pursue it further on his own account. I must content myself here with indicating logic and mathematics as spheres of truth and understanding which it is exceptionally hard to bring within empiricist terms.

Is not this also true of our judgments of worth and kindred matters in morals and aesthetics? We certainly do require knowledge of facts in these cases, but must we not have more? Am I, for example, to work for the abolition of capital punishment? To answer I must consider whether there are likely to be more murders if this punishment is stopped and whether the lives of policemen are put in jeopardy and so forth. But I must also believe that human life is worth preserving and have some more detailed notion also of what counts in human life. At some point I must pass some judgment on the facts. I may know, for example, that some act will cause pain, but how do I know that it is wrong to cause pain when this does not lead to some compensating good? Answers have been given in terms of our own reactions, the rules and conventions of society, our basic commitments and so on. But those who do not find these 'naturalistic' answers satisfactory will find in ethical judgments at some point a factor which goes beyond empiricist terms of any kind. The same is true in aesthetics. In judging a work of art we certainly must know properly what it is like; it is an advantage to have our attention drawn to features of a poem or painting which we are apt to overlook, and the art critic can do much to help us here. But it is not enough to know what the poem is like, for its beauty belongs to the poem in virtue of what it is, but is also more than what the poem itself is. If this something more is not just our feelings or some other attitude of ours, it looks as if the beauty of the poem involves something more than the facts of what things are like.

All these are difficult and highly controversial matters. A proper study of them would require at least one book to itself. At the moment it must suffice to give these further indications of points where the critics of empiricism feel that this kind of philosophy is put to considerable strain. A similar point is found when we think of the self or the soul. It may be that we only know other persons by observation of their behaviour, but does not their behaviour disclose to us something 'inner' akin to what we find ourselves, in direct experience of ourselves, to be? This is also a most controversial matter at present, and anyone who wishes to mount a full-scale attack on empiricism is bound to have a great deal to say about it. Perhaps it is here more than anywhere that the most certain limit of empiricism is reached.

It should be added that in seeking to meet the claims of the empiricist, and above all in considering fairly what makes them plausible, we learn a good deal about the way to present other positions. We shall not, for example, if we have learnt our lesson, speak too crudely of the self as if it were just like some object in the external world and we shall avoid such pitfalls and travesties as those involved in much loose talk about 'a realm of values' and so on. We acquire more of the caution and subtlety which is needed for a truly philosophical handling of various matters, this being one of the main ways in which philosophical controversy advances the subject.

I do not, however, wish to undertake here a close examination of empiricism. It must be enough to indicate some of the main ways in which its opponents have found it wanting. But one point should be noted. It is that in seeking to rebut empiricist claims in the respects just noted one does so by controverting them fairly directly, that is we expressly affirm that the empiricist is altogether wrong about certain matters, there are things we all recognize, however hard to understand in some ways, which seem to be beyond the limits the empiricist sets himself. In religion the position is more subtle, and although we pass here, in my view, more certainly than anywhere beyond the limits of empiricism, there is also more to be learnt in religion from taking the full impact of the criticisms advanced by empiricism today.

This is because there is some point in religion where we seem to pass, not merely beyond the sort of facts the empiricist can admit, but beyond all that we encounter in our experience of the world and in our understanding of it – and of ourselves. At the heart of religion there is, as a rule at least, some reference to a reality 'beyond', and in most cases this 'beyond' is understood in a very strict sense. There is a God who is not in time but eternal and uncreated, absolute and without limit. He may be thought of in personal or theistic terms as is common in the West, but we may also be told more vaguely still of the Supreme Self, the One, the Ultimate, which has none of the limitations to which we are subject. But what sense can we make of this? If the God we are to worship is altogether 'beyond' the sort of experience of things we have, if he is perfect in such a way that none of our conceptions apply to him, how can he come within our thoughts at all? Must he not remain an unfathomable mystery? But if he is such a mystery can we even say that he exists?

This is not a new problem. Thinkers have been acutely aware of it down the ages. But it has been very much sharpened of late. This has come about when empiricists have pressed upon us the question of how religious affirmations are verified. Their presupposition has been that the verification must be in terms of some natural or other observable reality of the kind which the scientist studies. We have seen reason to question this presupposition. None the less a problem remains. For, granted that there is more to the life and experience we have than the empiricist admits, we have only to broaden the question and ask what the test of truth can be for affirmations which pass altogether beyond the sort of reality we meet in experience and which our minds are capable of handling. We cannot meet the infinite or unlimited Being as if it were some specific or limited entity within the world: the Creator is not part of the world he has created. But in what other way can God be met and known? By putting the question insistently in their own restricted terms the empiricists have forced us to become more acutely conscious than ever of a problem which lives at the centre of religious thought and which is inescapable whether we are verificationists in the strict contemporary sense or not.

The accentuation of the problem in question, and with that an exceptionally shrewd appreciation of the way it should be met, marks, in my opinion, a major advance in religious understanding today; and this illustrates well how advance is made in philosophy by sharp controversy and heed to the insights found in positions with which we may not have much sympathy. The defender of religion owes much to his empiricist critics today at the point where his own thought can be most constructive.

This comes about especially when persistent critical questioning forces many to abandon the half-way houses in which they might otherwise seek a less disconcerting place in which to rest. For there are many who would not, on the one hand, wish to come to terms with empiricism but who are averse, on the other hand, to making the object of worship in religion so different from anything else we encounter that it seems to elude us altogether and have no relevance to the life we lead now. They thus tend to represent God, or whatever takes his place in their religion, as a spiritual reality far exceeding what we find in fact in the world, around us and in human life, but not altogether different in nature from other finite things. This is sometimes described as the theory of a 'finite God'. One of the main attractions of this theory is that it makes it easier in one respect to deal with the age-long problem of evil, that is the problem of accounting for various forms of evil in a world alleged to be under the control of a Perfect Being. For while we would still say that God is 'all-good' we can now add that there are some things which thwart him – at least over a period. He is not strictly all-powerful. This however does not accord well with what religious people feel. They tend to feel they can rest in the absolute goodness of God as being also superior to all ills, although it does not come within their comprehension how this can be. It is moreover very hard to show waht reason there can be for believing in a finite God. The way things happen in the world does not require us to postulate him. There may be creatures in the universe superior to ourselves. But have we any firm evidence of their existence?

The case for there being at least one overwhelmingly superior but not absolute being is usually made to rest on the presence of design or order in the universe and the preponderance of good. This is known as the 'teleological argument' for the existence of God. At the moment it must suffice to note that it has little appeal to thinkers of any school today. Perhaps there are features of it that have more relevance than we realize. But in general it has been largely discredited because critical thinkers have argued that if we are to proceed along the lines suggested we must observe the same standards of evidence in principle as we require in seeking to establish the existence of the sort of entities we normally find in the world. The movement of thought involved is the same. But when the alleged evidence is considered it is found to be vague and uncertain and, on some presentations of it, to amount to no more than indications of interesting features of the world from which nothing in particular can be inferred.

It is also urged that the attitude adopted by religious people is usually sharply at odds with the uncertain and tentative character of the teleological argument and kindred reflections. At the centre of his religion, although not always elsewhere, the worshipper normally claims an unshakable certainty. He does not just hope, he believes without shadow of doubt. 'I know', not 'I opine', or 'it seems likely', is the basic language of religion. And what is known is, moreover, not just some reality superior to ourselves, a being much greater in power and wisdom, but some altogether Supreme Reality, an infinite, eternal or absolute Being, one who is not in any way subject to our limitations but perfect and self-contained in a way that is not possible for finite entities like ourselves and all that we find in the world around us.

This is the central point of the insistence that 'no man hath seen God', that 'His ways are not our ways', that God is inscrutable and beyond our comprehension, and it is in the context of thought of this kind that we encounter perplexing doctrines such as the notion that God is one God but also three persons. It is not expected that we should be capable of rationalizing these notions and explaining closely and exhaustively what they mean. They belong to 'the mysteries of faith'.

Our critics have, on the one hand, forced us to be more unambiguous and explicit about this central and exceedingly perplexing aspect of religion. They have done so in part by noting that this is how religious people have generally thought and spoken, they have brought us back from what, in more rationalist moods, we would like religion to be and made us more conscious of its true accents, not in variable incidentals but at the heart of it. But it has also been urged relentlessly that the attempts to reason our way from the facts of the world as we find it, including its more distinctive and significant features, to some superior reality akin in nature to itself have the faults already noted. Nothing seems to be explained in these terms which could not be better explained otherwise. The evidence is either meagre or so qualified as to yield no distinctive result.

Contemporary criticism has not only forced the religious apologist to regard the object of worship in religion, and the basis of the saint's sense of absolute security, as being in some way altogether beyond the world as we comprehend it, an eternal uncreated reality, it has also insisted with equal vigour that a reality which falls so completely outside the sphere in which our own minds are at home can mean nothing to us. If we affirm that God is not known as other things are known, if there is no inference to him from the way the world goes, if he stands in no specific relation to other entities and does not admit of being known and characterized in that way, does it make sense to suppose that we know him at all? In short, if we say that God is a total mystery we may have well evaded one horn of the attack upon us but only to be firmly impaled on another; we have no longer to provide reasons for believing in God and make these run the gauntlet of criticism, but has not the affirmation which remains been emptied of all content and significance? We cannot think a total mystery, and in insisting that we indicate how our affirmations are understood and what considerations, whether strictly empiricist or not, are relevant to their appraisal, our critics seem to have closed with particular firmness the only avenue of escape that seems possible. I submit, all the same, that by forcing us ruthlessly into this particular dilemma they have done us a great service and opened out for us the way to real understanding. His comments on 'Post-Copernican man' are developed at length in *What is Man?* (SCM Press, 1970), one of a series of studies of contemporary theological issues published under the title of 'centrebooks'.

Like H. D. Lewis, **David Jenkins**, Director of the *Humanum* Studies Project at the World Council of Churches, Geneva, is also unwilling to concede ground unnecessarily to the critics of Christianity. Writing against the background of the Honest to God debate, he is chiefly concerned to ask the right questions, and his list of areas in which this might profitably be done includes some which theologians, including several represented here, have tended to dismiss. The historical points he makes are outlined at greater length in his *Guide to the Debate about God* (Lutterworth Press, 1966), and his questioning is taken further in his Bampton Lectures, *The Glory of Man* (SCM Press, 1967) and *Living with Questions* (SCM Press, 1969).

David Jenkins · *Whither the Doctrine of God Now?*

This paper does not get nearly far enough. But I do not believe we have yet gone deep enough in diagnosing the situation with regard to the doctrine of God. Until this is done we cannot see anything clearly about where the doctrine of God should go. Hence this paper is intended as a contribution to the future development of the doctrine of God by being an attempt to diagnose the present situation more clearly.

The question has been raised as to whether we are or ought to be in sight of the end of theism. Theism would come to an end if one of two mutually exclusive sets of conditions obtained. The first possibility is that there is no God and that everyone comes to realize this. Theism is thus known to be void, ceases to exercise any hold and fades completely away. The second possibility is that the Christian symbol of the Last Day stands for that which will be realized in the eventual experience of all men. In that 'event' men would 'in the End' see God with an immediacy which is best described as 'face to face' and theism would be shattered not because it was voided but because it was fulfilled. The point is that theism does not exist in its own right. It is either totally superstition or a body of belief, understanding and practice which in some form or other is required by the intermediate and interim nature of our situation and our experience. Theism is either mistaken about reality or else properly expectant about reality. In neither case is it completely and straightforwardly descriptive of reality.

Our present debate, however, is immediately occasioned by some who, while intending to remain Christians, wish to deny the continuing validity of some clear and exhaustive distinction between the positions of theism and atheism as just touched on. In raising the question 'The end of Theism?', Bishop Robinson clearly did not think he was pointing to either of the possibilities referred to above. Rather he was suggesting that the symbol of a transcendent and personal God which was the essence of theism had indeed now turned out to be superstitious. That is, this symbol not only did not correspond in any understandable or life-enhancing way with reality, but was positively misleading and mythological about reality. Thus, if modern 'believers' are to continue to keep hold of those features about reality for which the symbols of theism had once stood, and if others are to be helped to come to grips with those aspects, it is necessary to recognize the end of theism. We must face the possibility of abandoning the symbols of theism associated with and focused upon that of the personal and transcendent God and find other ways of talking and organizing our experience. None the less, this is not a programme for atheism. It is aiming at some third thing which would rescue theism from superstition, and atheism from unbelief. Reluctant believers and enthusiastic unbelievers, however, tend to refuse to accept this and hold that the programme does look, logically, like a programme for atheism.

For reasons which will, I hope, appear, I agree with this diagnosis. For theism to come to an end in this world would only leave everyone as atheists. But it will merely encourage everyone to become or remain atheist if atheistic believers do not face up to the reasons which prompted that sort of an attempt to find a third way (between theism and atheism) of which Robinson has given us an example. In this connection there are two sets of considerations, the first to do with the climate of thought in which theism is to be entertained as a live option, and the second to do with the manner in which a theistic position has in fact been occupied and maintained over a very large range of recent and general Christian thought and practice.

With regard to the climate of thought, I wish to focus on what seems to me to be the crucial point for the development of theology by talking of 'Post-Copernican Man'. I choose this symbol from Kant's preface to the second edition of his *Critique of Pure Reason* and I do so because I believe that Kant rightly perceived the inwardness and the implications of the revolution in thought which modern man was producing and which was producing modern man.

Kant was concerned 'to introduce a complete revolution in the procedure of metaphysics, after the example of the Geometricians and the Natural Philosophers'. He proposed 'to do just what Copernicus did in attempting to explain the celestial movements. When he found that he could make no progress by assuming that all the heavenly bodies revolved around the spectator he reversed the process and tried the experiment of assuming that the spectator revolved while the stars remained at rest.' In this Copernicus was typical of the various experimentalists who had 'learned that reason only perceives that which it produces after its own design, that it must not be content to follow, as it were, in the leading-strings of nature but must . . . compel nature to reply to its questions'. Kant saw that this revolution in thought about the world (the replacement of the objective knower with his divine gift of reason by the subjective observer with the human capacity for experiment) required a revolution in thought about thought. Men did not gain their knowledge by the pure and *a priori* use of a reason which had the intrinsic capacity of penetrating through the appearances of phenomena to the ultimate realities. It was no longer one's understanding of reality which determined one's articulation and assessment of the observed appearances. Rather one's observation and articulation of the appearances were on the way to becoming that which determined one's understanding of reality.

It is necessary to say 'on the way to becoming' when we are at Kant's stage and part in the revolution because, as is well known, Kant himself held that while the speculative reason could not go beyond its own categories and the phenomena, practical reason took one validly into the sphere of reality in which talk about God, Free Will and Goodness was proper, necessary and truthful. Here Kant remains a believer in transcendental reality, to the knowledge of which he held that the practical reason could build a rational bridge.

Post-Copernican Man in his maturity has not allowed Kant's revolution in philosophy to stem the whole revolution and preserve the transcendent realities in the manner Kant himself intended. He has carried through the revolution in thinking about the world and in thinking about thought to the completion of a revolution in the understanding of understanding itself and of knowledge. The result is that the first question which must be faced in any serious and relevant attempt to maintain, develop, re-state, or even re-establish a doctrine of God is not 'Is there a God?' or 'What is meant by "God"?' but 'What is it to know?' For the answer to that question implies and presupposes an answer to the question 'What can be known?', i.e. 'What can, with reasonable confidence, be held to be real?' or, even, 'What is real and how is it real?' The spirit in which Post-Copernican

Man explicitly or implicitly answers such questions is well reflected, for example, in the definition which Professor D. R. Newth gives (in his contribution to *Science and its Context*, ed. J. Brierley) of science as 'the process by which men create knowledge in which they can place a high and often measurable degree of confidence'. Knowledge is that which is produced by the use of the experimental method when men 'compel nature to reply to . . . questions' (*vide* Kant cit. *supra*). Such knowledge is firm and can be confidently used, although it is never 'final' in more than a strictly limited sense. As Heisenberg says (*The Physicist's Conception of Nature*, pp. 27 f.): 'In the exact sciences the word "final" obviously means that there are always self-contained, mathematically representable, systems of concepts and laws applicable to certain realms of experience, in which realms they are always valid. . . Obviously, however, we cannot expect these concepts and laws to be suitable for the subsequent description of new realms of experience.' A little later he remarks: 'The exact sciences also start from the assumption that in the end it will always be possible to understand nature, even in every new field of experience, but that we may make no *a priori* assumptions about the meaning of the word "understand".'

Knowledge is a strictly human achievement which is strictly limited and relative, but which is none the less extremely potent within its limits, not least because these limits are precisely known. For Post-Copernican Man knowledge is the articulated understanding of observable and measurable realities so far achieved. There is more to know by the same and developed techniques. As such knowledge is gained it will change our understanding of what has hitherto been known. Truth is relative and it becomes truth as it is discovered, established, put to the test, articulated and used as the basis for further discovery, further relative but relevant truth. You cannot 'go beyond' the knowledge you have save by building on what you have got in strict continuity with it. Experience, experiment and techniques for testing by application in understanding and action are the tests of knowledge and thereby of reality.

The symbol 'Post-Copernican Man' as representing the attitude to knowledge and reality not very precisely indicated above is, I believe, a more useful representation for our purpose in considering theism than the vaguer 'modern man', for the symbolism draws attention to the fact that the crisis for belief is, at its centre, epistemological – to do with knowing and what is knowable. Further, anyone who embodies or expresses the qualities and approach symbolized by Post-Copernican Man has today an unquestioned authority, an authority which is believed to be self-evident. Any other approach will not be heeded unless it can give a very good account of itself in terms which at least overlap those of Post-Copernican Man and which can establish their own claim to relevant meaningfulness. This is why Robinson attempted a version of what I have called the third way. Theism (belief in and talk about a transcendent and personal God) goes beyond the knowable facts. Theism is therefore not knowledge concerned with reality. Once it was symbolism referring mythologically to features of reality but now, on Post-Copernican principles, it is seen to be superstition and must therefore come to an end. The features of reality the symbols of theism used to refer to must be found now more firmly located in 'real' reality, i.e. that which is now known and judged to be knowable. Hence the programme to re-express theism in terms of depth, concern, encounter and relationships.

But, understandable as such a programme is, it is not really a programme to replace outmoded symbols. The trouble about symbols is only symptomatic of the real trouble, which is that about knowledge and reality. For the programme is an attempt to come to terms with Post-Copernican Man on his terms and these do not envisage the possibility of there being a reality which can only, and must always, be pointed to by symbols. That which is real is that which is known and that which is known is that which has been described. There is always more to know, but we shall know this when we are able to describe more. Knowledge and reality remain relative terms. Hence if theism is to become acceptable to Post-Copernican Man it must become atheism, i.e. it must surrender to him, for he has no terms for anything other than relative reality and relative truth. Whatever the symbols of theism stood for, they stood for something that was in logic (and, the theist contends, in reality) different from anything which falls within the logical possibilities of Post-Copernican Man's terms. For the theist, the significance of God's presence, immanence, availability is always derived from otherness and his absoluteness. This is a matter not of mythology, but of logic. Part of the confusion in *Honest to God* and in much of the current debate is the failure to recognize this. Anyone concerned with the future of the Doctrine of God must face up to the starkness of the clash involved here. Concentrating on symbols can simply disguise the fact that the full development of the approach of Post-Copernican Man to the world is literally godless. Symbolism is certainly a question for the doctrine of God but only after, or at least as part of, the answer to the question as to how a Doctrine of God is to be maintained and commended in a world where the acceptedly authoritative man is godless.

I have spent half of this article seeking to define more clearly what seems to me to be the essential nature of the challenge now presented to theism and to make clear how stark and definite a challenge it is because I am myself sure that the future of theism, the direction for the development of the doctrine of God, is to be found in facing up with accuracy and rigour to the challenge of the situation. This is a theological conclusion from my present understanding of the doctrine of God and it is reached as follows.

Any doctrine of God which is in continuity with the theism of the Bible and of Christian tradition must be clear about at least the following. *First*, the word 'God' refers to, or, better, names (a) reality who/which is other than the sum total of the realities which constitute the observable (or theoretically observable) universe.

The being named 'God' is not simply different *from* other beings or realities. He is different *in* being and reality. That is the logical point indicated by the caution which has to be used in referring to him as *a* being. That is also why he can be referred to only in symbols, analogies, etc. To use the name 'God' and to believe that one is using it meaningfully is to assert that the reality of the world is not exhausted by the realities in the world and that symbols of the type 'out there', 'beyond this', 'on another level', or the like (logically like, that is) are inescapable if we are to attempt to do justice to the reality in which we are involved. It is also why the conflict between Post-Copernican Man and the theist is logical with the certainty that one position or other in its ultimate conclusion about the world is false, rather than mythological with the hope that a third way would resolve the conflict. The debate is not about talk but about the way things really are. Thus the radical otherness of God (in a logical, ontological and existential sense) is a theistic axiom.

Secondly, however, the theist in the biblical and Christian tradition holds that this is no absolute bar to the knowledge of God because God related himself to the world and to man. The symbols which refer to this relationship are primarily 'Creation' and 'Revelation'. The symbol of Creation stands for the assertion of the fact as a fact that the existence of realities other than God is ultimately dependent upon God. Therefore, it is conceivably in the nature of things that these other realities in their own reality may reflect God or be usable as a means of communication about God or even of God. The symbol of Revelation stands for the assertion of the fact that God so relates himself to the world that he evokes knowledge of himself in, and in connection with, particular persons and events.

Now this belief in, and assertion about, God as reality, who is both other and at the same time related as Creator and Revealer, seems to have been almost completely thrown on the defensive by a full and open confrontation with Post-Copernican Man. In this defensiveness theism is false to its own premises and experience. This brings us to the second set of considerations related to the future of the Doctrine of God – those to do with the manner in which Christian theism has very largely been practised and the doctrine of God taught as men have moved into the Post-Copernican era. There has been a widespread failure either to teach sufficiently radically about, or take practical notice of, the fact that theism does not exist in its own right. It has been unconsciously assumed that, on the basis of a taken-for-granted authority of the Bible and/or the Church, talk about

God would remain both meaningful and relevant in its own right. But religious symbols which are taken for granted and left to have force in their own right and by their own weight become idols. The very name of God is only too easily taken in vain and the repeated sin of religious men is to rely on their religion (their concepts and their rules) rather than on the God to whom the symbols pointed and with whom the religion was validly concerned. Symbols are inescapably necessary in theism. But they operate only as stultifying idols unless they are used in a manner which is not self-contained but open. God is radically other. Therefore, the truth about him or the reality of him cannot be contained in or be equivalent to any particular set of symbols, symbolic acts or significant encounters. All such may be means of knowing God but are not to be equated with God.

But God is related and present as Creator and Revealer. Hence the Universe is always furnished with potential symbols, and the possibilities of symbolic acts and opportunities for encounter which can kindle and have kindled the knowledge of God. Hence when theism is threatened and much (or even all) of the symbolism seems to be going dead the believer in the God with whom the theistic tradition has to do will look for a renewal of theism. (He knows that, as there is God, theism cannot either fade away or be done without.) This renewal he will look for by seeking a greater openness to God. And *this* he will seek by a greater openness to the real (and not the supposed, muted or turned aside) challenge of the situation. For the God who is other is known in the intermediate and interim manner of theism through his presence and relatedness. And because God is real and is concerned with reality, he is not to be found in our illusions about the situation, but he is to be found as we seek to come to the closest grips we can with the objective reality of the situation.

It is here that the true concern of the theist meets up with the maturity of Post-Copernican Man. For Post-Copernican Man is determined to put everything to the test of experience and experiment and to proceed inductively from the knowledge he has to the building up of further knowledge. In fact, he is taking the givenness of what the theist would call the created universe absolutely seriously and in its own right. His ideal is to be open to observed and verified facts and thereby to dispel illusion and unclarity and to work in the light thus gained. This ideal represents an absolute commitment to pursuing the truth of the matter which is wholly proper to the givenness of a created universe, the data of which demand the respect which rejects all *a priori* treatment. The theist who believes that 'created' is a proper adjective to apply to the universe must not and cannot go back on this achievement of Post-Copernican Man in which he is more mature than theists have generally shown themselves to be.

What the theist knows is that there is also God to be known and that ultimately it is this knowledge which is both primary (God is the proper context of everything) and ultimate (God is the proper fulfilment of everything). He cannot, however, blame Post-Copernican Man for refusing to allow that he (the theist) has anything that can be called knowledge about 'God' if he neither behaves as if he has knowledge (i.e. does not approach given reality on the basis of a real – because competent and practical – understanding of something real) nor can give any reasonably plausible account of the source or bearing of his knowledge. The questions which Post-Copernican Man puts to the theist are 'How do you know God?' and 'How would you suggest to me that "knowledge of God" is knowledge?' These questions require answers based on experience (How was the body of knowledge built up and how is it passed on?) and related to possibilities of experimental living.

In facing this challenge of the situation, I would suggest, we are required to work our way towards a Post-Copernican natural theology, an account of revealed truth which is always sensitive to origins on the one hand and practical relevance on the other, and the development of a spiritual discipline and discipleship which is clearly an experimental attempt to make sense of our modern life in the light of our theistic understanding in the light of our modern life. In other words, there is no way forward in the doctrine of God save on the broadest of fronts and by combining a number of enterprises.

It may be thought that in my usage 'Post-Copernican natural theology' is a contradiction in terms, but I do not believe this is so. As a theist, I maintain the view that the universe is rightly characterized as 'created'. The experimental and inductive approach of Post-Copernican Man is the mature approach to the givenness of the created universe. If the theistic approach is in accord with the reality of things, then careful, sensitive and prolonged investigation of the methods, results and presuppositions of the Post-Copernican approach must yield material for a natural theology. It must be possible to find material to make a case for the 'theistic hypothesis', although it will never be possible to establish it finally. (This is where the other two aspects of the enterprise mentioned above come in.)

Among the areas for search may be included: epistemology itself (Logical Positivism is by no means as complete or satisfactory as some of its first proponents supposed or as some *avant-garde* but possibly behind the times theologians now suppose. Also pure existentialism may perhaps without much difficulty be shown to lead to 'the Absurd'); freedom and morality (particularly the former where it may fairly speedily become evident that man cannot be established or maintained as human on strictly Post-Copernican principles. But in either field the insight of Kant – that here lies a bridge to the transcendent – needs to be vigorously explored); psychology and sociology (The more we know about individual and group features which affect and produce persons and personality, the more we may be able to see features in which self-contained descriptive and reductionist accounts of what personality is or what persons may be or may become are self-evidently unsatisfactory and incomplete. There is also the need to investigate and re-assess those ranges of human experience which Post-Copernican Man tries to undervalue or ignore in relation to knowledge and which have their revenge in producing a modern literature which is largely pessimistic, uncertain and unclear in contrast to Post-Copernican Man's certainty, clarity and optimism. But this again must be investigated in its own right and not be prostituted and distorted by being prematurely forced into ready-made theological categories (re guilt, sin and the like). The natural theology must be built up from what is observed in the natural as it is given to us.

But this search for a Post-Copernican natural theology would never be undertaken nor would it have any hope of success if it were not the case that there existed a reliable tradition of revealed knowledge of God and a constant community of current experience recognizably continuous with the experience of those who were the means of producing the tradition. God is to be known in and through the realities of the situation, but God is not the same thing as the situation, the otherness remains a reality. Natural theology can aim at showing that there is a possibility of God in the situation. But to look for a possibility of God one must have some idea of what 'God' could mean and this comes from a sensitive and lively confrontation with the tradition in which one begins to separate the symbols from the logic, and the mythology from the experience. It is to this end that the tradition, whether in the Bible or in doctrinal formulations or in the worshipping and praying practice of Christians, is to be studied and sifted with particular regard to origins (the situations which gave rise to the tradition) and relevance (the way situations were held to be affected by that which was formulated into tradition). (Here particular attention will have to be given to the data of and about the historical Jesus. I would venture the prophecy that more can reasonably be known in this field than the present prevailing fashions in exegesis will allow, overwhelmed as they are by a probably unsound existentialist epistemology. There may well be sufficient facts of a 'hard' (by Post-Copernican standards) sort about Jesus to go quite a long way in legitimately raising the question as to whether the reality of the world is contained in and exhausted by the realities in the world.)

But that which convinces the theist that there is a God and that the challenge of Post-Copernican Man is a challenge to learn more of God and not a summons to fight a rearguard action on God's (doubtful) behalf are the occasions, whether individual or corporate, whether vivid or faintly and evasively remembered, when the challenge of the situation and the givenness of the Tradition are kindled into an awareness which makes practical, comforting and illuminating sense of both, by giving what must be described as the knowledge of a Presence and a Power. Hence it is that no doctrine of God can go forward unless it is clearly related to a spiritual discipline and discipleship which is experiential and experimental in relation both to the tradition and to the current situation.

Thus the future of the development of the doctrine of God must lie in sustained attempts to give an account of the ways in which confrontation of the situation, exploration of the tradition and personal discipleship yield knowledge of God and what the content and bearing of this knowledge is. Such attempts must emerge from and be backed up by a Christian community which is plainly living experimentally and openly. The challenge of Post-Copernican Man has decisively reminded us that Christian theology and Christian living must be conducted together.

Finally, **John Macquarrie**, Lady Margaret Professor of Divinity in the University of Oxford, places the whole of theology in a wider context. Professor Macquarrie has written a series of books which make rich use of the approach discussed in the second section above (see especially *Principles of Christian Theology*, SCM Press, 1966) as well as a comprehensive account of *Twentieth Century Religious Thought* (SCM Press, 1963). This essay, taken from *Studies in Christian Existentialism* (SCM Press, 1966), is a reminder on the one hand, to the church, that it needs theology if it is to be true to its calling, and on the other, to the theologian, that his work is misguided if it is not done in the service of the church.

John Macquarrie · *The Service of Theology*

The very title of this essay may occasion some lifting of eyebrows. Is not theology the most authoritarian of subjects? Has it not consistently sought to be the master rather than the servant? Does it not lay down dogmas to which men are expected to conform? And whatever the word 'dogma' may have signified originally or however it may be understood among professional theologians, has it not now acquired in ordinary usage the meaning assigned to it in one of our leading English dictionaries: 'an arrogant declaration of opinion'?

There was a time, so we are told, when theology was the most venerated of all branches of study, but that time is long since past, and today its stock has fallen very low. Theology is despised by those who stand outside of the Church. They doubt whether it is a genuine branch of serious study at all. They question whether it should still be taught in our universities. They remember that theologians have in the past interfered with the progress of various sciences, and tried to impede them. They cannot see that theology has any service to render. Moreover, theology is also despised by many people within the Church. When the average congregation is looking for a new minister, it rarely attaches much importance to theological qualifications. It looks for a popular preacher, an active pastor, an able organizer, but it mistrusts the so-called 'academic' type, for it must be acknowledged that theology often seems as remote and useless to the ordinary church member as it does to the secularist.

These considerations, however, merely show that theology, like everything else, can become perverted. If theology sets itself up as a heterogeneous collection of infallible information about every subject under the sun, then it rightly earns the contempt of the scientist. And if it should happen, as James I. McCord has recently expressed it, that theology gets 'divorced from the life of the Church' and 'has been betrayed into sterile intellectualism and scholasticism', then it is rightly suspect in the eyes of the ordinary church member. It would seem therefore that before we can properly discuss the service of theology, we must be clear about what theology is and about what it is not.

A book such as H. R. Mackintosh's *Types of Modern Theology* illustrates the bewildering variety of forms which theology may take – and of course there are other forms besides those which Mackintosh considers, some of which have emerged even in the generation or so that has elapsed since his book was written. Underlying each type of theology there is a distinctive conception of what theology is. How are we to decide which is the correct conception – indeed, how are we to know whether there is any one correct conception? Perhaps there are different styles of theology, just as there are different styles of art, and perhaps each one can claim its right and justification. It may help if we consider briefly two extreme points of view.

On the one hand, some apologists have made the claim that theology is an empirical science. They endeavour to narrow the gap between theology and other branches of learning, to minimize the offence which theology gives to the secularist, and to argue that as an empirical science theology is as securely based as any other empirical science, and has as much claim to a place in the spectrum of university studies. Superficially, the word 'theology' looks much the same as the word 'geology'. One would mean 'discourse about God' and the other 'discourse about the earth'. But whereas the earth is visible, tangible and generally accessible to the senses, God is not so. The similarity of designation between the two branches of inquiry conceals a radical difference. The claim that theology is an empirical science affords a good example of an apparently important assertion which, on examination, needs to be qualified to such an extent that the original claim is eroded away to something relatively insignificant. When we examine the claim about theology, we find that it involves a twofold equivocation. There is firstly an ambiguity in the adjective 'empirical'. As commonly used nowadays, this adjective is applied to that which can somehow be tested by sense experience; but as the apologist who claims that theology is an empirical science uses the word, the meaning is qualified or stretched to cover experiences which are allegedly non-sensory. Secondly, there is a similar ambiguity in the noun 'science'.

W. C. Dampier is perhaps not far from common usage when he defines 'science' as 'ordered knowledge of natural phenomena' (*A History of Science* (3rd ed.; London: Cambridge University Press, 1942), p. xiii), but the apologist who claims that theology is a science will usually also lay claim to a knowledge of more than natural phenomena, and he must once more stretch the meaning of the term which he uses. I do not wish to deny that a wider meaning can be given to the expression 'empirical science' than that which is commonly given, or even that it may be unfortunate that the range of 'empirical' and 'science' has been narrowed down in modern times. But I do wish to point out that, in view of the current usage of words, it is so highly misleading to speak of theology as an 'empirical science' as to be almost positively incorrect; and by the time the misapprehensions have been removed by the suitable qualification of both the adjective and the noun, the original assertion has become quite shadowy and probably unimportant. Nothing is to be gained by minimizing the difference between theology and all other '-ologies'. Such a procedure can only be irritating to the philosopher and the scientist, and confusing to the theologian himself. We must clearly recognize that theology is somehow *different* from other branches of learning.

At the opposite extreme, there are those who think of theology as a purely esoteric body of knowledge. This knowledge is claimed to be based on a divine revelation, and is held to be completely discontinuous with any other knowledge that we may have. It is self-contained and self-authenticating, it can be neither confirmed nor disproved by human reason, and the extreme advocates of this point of view seem to claim that it can indulge freely in paradox and antinomy, and it can even rejoice in absurdity. But supposing that what we get to know through divine revelation is 'wholly other' or 'qualitatively different' from what we get to know in other ways, the knowing is not itself qualitatively different from other knowing – if it were, we could not speak of 'knowing'. Such knowledge could not even *contradict* our natural knowledge unless it were in logical relations with it. Divine revelation is presumably something which is unique in its nature, and calls into play a special mode of knowing. Theology, however, as reflection upon the explication of such revelation, is not identical with the revelation. It is a branch of inquiry which must have regard for logic, and part of its task is to clarify the relations between what it claims to know and what we get to know in other disciplines. The theologian, if he is not going to live in a private world, must be prepared somewhere to emerge from the circle of theological ideas. If he gains nothing by minimizing the difference between his subject and other branches of study, he loses everything by making that difference absolute. It is part of his service – and this at least is implied in the name 'theo*logy*' – to make his discourse as intelligible as possible (*pace* Kierkegaard and the 'knight of faith').

Theology, we have argued so far, is different from what is commonly called an 'empirical science', and yet it is not so different that there can be no relation between theology and other fields of knowledge. We must now try to work out these characteristics of theology in such a way as to arrive at a clearer understanding both of the nature of a genuine theological inquiry, and of the service which it renders.

Let us suppose that an overseas visitor to England is watching a game of cricket for the first time in his life. He sees one man bowling the ball, and another hitting it with his bat, he sees the batsmen running the length of the pitch and running back again, he sees the field changing over, and it all means nothing to him. And when the batsman steps out of his crease and pats a few blades of grass with the back of his bat, the visitor is completely mystified. Nothing in the game has any significance for him, and he wonders why the British are able to work up such enthusiasm for it. In such cases, we would attempt an explanation. We might get a book of rules and instruct the visitor in them. These rules tell us how the game is actually played. When we had got to the end ofthem, the visitor might say, 'Well, I begin to see what they are doing, and that there is some method in their madness, but nevertheless I think it is a remarkably stupid game.' If we ourselves, however, were cricketers, we might feel that he was hardly as yet qualified to pass so sweeping a judgment, and we might pass on to a different kind of explanation. We could put a bat in his hand, stand him at the wicket and send down a few balls – in other words, we could induce him to participate in the game. Only then, the cricketer would maintain, could our visitor begin to understand properly what this game really is – what it demands in the way of alertness, what skills it develops, and so forth. Possibly the visitor might become interested and begin to share something of the enthusiasm of the players. But if he still thought it a very stupid game, it is hard to see what more could be done for him and it would seem that we would have to give up trying to explain.

To the outside observer in the twentieth century, the life, work and worship of the Christian Church may seem as odd and unintelligible as the game of cricket to the visitor in our analogy. Once again, of course, it is possible to give some kind of explanation from the outside. The observer can be instructed in the history of religion and in the development of Christianity as a historical phenomenon. He can be instructed in the psychology of religion and shown the ways in which religious attitudes originate. These subjects do, in fact, have their place in any study of religion. But when everything has been said that can be said under these headings, we have still only scraped the surface of the problem of explanation. We have still not arrived at theology, in the proper sense.

Theological explanation is of the second kind mentioned in our analogy – it is explanation which necessarily involves participation. It is from the inside, not from the outside. This is the point at which the theologian is in a radically different position from the natural scientist. The scientist is, so far as possible (and this qualification is demanded because it may be that all knowing involves some degree of participation), detached from his subject-matter and aims at purely objective description. The theologian is dealing with something that can be understood only through becoming involved in it. It is not just an accident of style that in some of the greatest theologians of the Church, such as St Augustine and St Anselm, we find that prayer and exposition stand side by side in their writings and that they pass almost imperceptibly from the one to the other. Theology is grounded in faith; it is faith expressing itself, faith making itself articulate.

It need hardly be said that, in the New Testament sense of the word, 'faith' does not stand for a mere belief. Faith includes belief, but it includes also obedience. It is an attitude of the whole personality. Hence arises one of the peculiar characteristics of theological language which, as some of our logical analysts express it, is at once descriptive and prescriptive. That is to say that it does not deal with intellectual abstractions but always relates to the concrete situations in which men live and act and choose. It may be recalled that in the exchange of correspondence which took place between Adolf von Harnack and Karl Barth in 1923, one of Harnack's accusations was to the effect that Barth was transforming theology from a science into a form of preaching. Perhaps these men represented extreme positions, but Barth was right in so far as he saw that a genuine theology cannot be just an academic study of religion but is rather the explication of a faith by which men live. Preaching, in its turn, as the proclamation of the acts on which the faith of the Church rests, must be theological if it is to be more than an emotional appeal or entertaining rhetoric. The congregation which is looking for a popular non-theological preacher does not want a preacher at all.

Because it is rooted in faith, theology is a necessary part of the Church's service. Like all other Christian service, it is at once a gift and a task. The knowledge which comes with faith is described in the New Testament as a gift of the Spirit: 'The revelation of the Spirit is imparted to each, to make the best advantage of it. One learns to speak with wisdom, by the power of the Spirit, another to speak with knowledge, with the same Spirit for his rule' (1 Cor. 12.7–8). Yet the Christian who has received such a gift of the Spirit has a duty to grow 'richer and richer yet, in the fulness of its knowledge and the depth of its perception' (Phil. 1.9). The service of theology is to pursue and promote this growth in the knowledge and understanding of Christian faith. The faith of the ordinary church member is often implicit rather than explicit. Situations arise in which he needs guidance. Theology is serving the Church when it makes clear the bearing of the Christian faith in such situations, and theology itself is never in danger of becoming 'academic' in the bad sense so long as it keeps in touch with these situations. St Paul's theological insights find expression in letters written to help the local churches with their problems, and theological advance has taken place since his time wherever the faith has been interpreted and elucidated in relation to the Church's concrete problems, needs and opportunities.

The situations will be of many kinds, and the questions will arise in varying contexts. They may arise in the field of doctrine, as with the advent of a hostile philosophy, such as Marxism; or in the field of church order, as in efforts toward reunion; in the field of personal conduct, as in the face of new moral problems such as those presented by techniques of contraception and artificial insemination; or in the field of social ethics, as in the matter of racial tensions. The boundaries between systematic theology, practical theology and Christian ethics are fluid, but in each case the service of theology is the same – to enable the Church to see each question clearly in the light of the revelation of God in Christ.

Although I have laid considerable stress on the need for theology to be related to the life and experience of the Church, this should not be taken to imply a completely subservient attitude. It may sometimes be the duty of theology to criticize accepted beliefs or practices of the Church. The internal criticism is itself a service, and so that it can be properly exercised, the Church should ensure all reasonable freedom in theological discussion.

Up till now I have spoken of the service which theology renders within the Church. I seem to have left aside the visitor from overseas in our analogy, the man who had no conception of cricket at all. Has theology any service to give to those who are outside of the Church? Of course, it could be said that in so far as theology serves the Church in the ways already described, it indirectly serves the larger needs of the world by contributing to the witness which the Church bears in its preaching and in its life. Theology has its part in that prophetic ministry in which the Church speaks forth to the world. But is there not a more direct way in which theology may serve those who are outside of the Church?

There is such a way, and it lies in that branch of theology which is usually called 'apologetics'. Yet here again the boundary-line between the several theological activities is not a hard-and-fast one. Dogmatics and apologetics cannot be sharply separated. Indeed, there is good theological precedent for the view that the Church and the world cannot be sharply separated, for the Church on earth is always a *corpus permixtum*, and the boundaries between the Church and the world are blurred. In so far as those within the Church are never sealed off from the prevalent secular thought of the age, they need an apologetic if they are to hold the faith firmly and intelligently in their generation. And in so far as there are many outside of the Church who are asking the kind of questions to which the Christian faith gives answers, they have that minimum of participation which is necessary to an understanding of the faith, if it is put to them in language the meaning of which they can grasp. While remaining true to the faith once delivered to the saints, theology must in its apologetic function find new terms, new ideas intelligible to the contemporary world, new cultural forms capable of making impact. It may borrow ideas from the current philosophy, and indeed theologians have done so from New Testament times onward. This does not imply a secularizing of Christian thought, though no doubt there is always the danger of distortion. What is aimed at is rather the Christianizing of current language and culture, and the dangers have to be faced. If theology shrinks from this wider service, then Christianity will increasingly become not a proclamation any more but a museum piece.

For there is a real danger that in our day Christianity may find itself not so much rejected as merely disregarded. This danger seems to me far more serious than the alleged danger of having Christian faith corrupted through alliances with modern philosophies. Since theology re-discovered its kerygmatic character a generation or so ago, it has tended to remain within the charmed circles of its own ideas. In the process, it has become more and more isolated. While this essay has fully conceded the difference between theology and other studies, it has also stressed that theology stands in relation to them. In the end, truth is one and our knowledge should be one. The theologian must step out of his circle. Surely we believe that the modern man to whom the Gospel is addressed should not be asked just to take a leap in the dark. He deserves to be shown, so far as it can be shown, that Christianity is a faith which can be reasonably held in the twentieth century. And who is to perform this service for him, unless it be the theologian? Admittedly there are difficulties which can only be solved *ambulando*, as one moves along in the life of faith, and admittedly there are mysteries which can never be fully penetrated. As has been fully recognized, understanding demands here some participation, and cannot be given in advance. But this by no means relieves the Church of removing preliminary obstacles to faith, by showing that the Christian message is not just a tissue of absurdities.

If I have in any way rightly described some of the tasks of the theologian, then he should be the last man to become arrogant or dogmatic, in the bad sense. He must rather be frightened by the responsibility that is laid upon him. He can only turn to his fellow servants in the Church and say: 'Pray for me too, that I may be given words to speak my mind boldly, in making known the Gospel revelation' (Eph. 6.19). His is no privileged position. Sometimes he will be tempted to pervert it. Often he will fall down on his task. But a genuine Christian theology, seeking as it does to interpret the revelation given in him who took the nature of a servant, is itself an essential service both to the Church of Christ and to mankind. Still more, it is a service to God, for the true science of God, as more than an intellectual discipline, leads to the love of God and is inseparable from it.

POSTSCRIPT

IN INDICATING the way forward for theology, the last section of this book made three important points. First, there must be continued searching into and examination of the resources of the Christian tradition to see in what ways it is still relevant for today. Second, Christian theology can never be simply a matter of talking; it must also be a form of doing as well, and if that is forgotten, both thought and action will become corrupted. Finally, despite the strength of the intellectual pressures against religious belief, it is still possible for a good case to be made out for a Christian faith which is in recognizable continuity with the past. The way in which these three points have been taken further in more recent theology will be the subject of this Postscript.

If the most recent writing on the nature of the Bible and Christian tradition is anything to go by, some aspects of Christian belief which have always been cornerstones in apologetics are not as secure as they were once thought to be. For along with a recognition of the importance of the past of Christianity for the present has come the realization that the past had only partial answers, even for its own time. Ronald Gregor Smith, Professor of Divinity at Glasgow University until his untimely death in 1969, in his important book *The Doctrine of God* (Collins, 1970), put the matter like this:

> All that comes to us out of the past, the whole *traditum* of the tradition, the creeds, the confessions, the deliverances of councils and assemblies, but also the rituals and liturgies, the hymns and the prayers and the uncountable treatises, tractates, broadsheets, the hardbacks and the paperbacks, concerning the Christian tradition: all, without any doubt, have

> their place. But they are not the truth. Even infinitesimally, they have their grain of truth. And even when their place is grand and assured, still it is only their few grains. At best, each points, in its own way, to the truth. They do not, even under the most propitious circumstances, possess the truth (p. 27).

Gregor Smith includes even the Bible under this judgment, pointing out that on closer inspection and by inescapable modern standards of literary and historical criticism, the order and clear line of Scripture are not so manifestly indisputable as the formulators of theories about Scripture once thought. And here he is supported by those who, on the strength of more than a century of biblical scholarship, have begun to put the question of the nature of the Bible in a new and pressing way.

It is characteristic, not only of the theology of the Word (see section 1 above), but of almost all modern continental theories of interpretation (certainly including Bultmann), to begin with the *datum* of the Bible, the historical canon, and to ask how it can be said to speak (or be made to speak) to men today. In his lecture 'The Use of the Bible in Modern Theology' (*Bulletin of the John Rylands Library* 52, Autumn 1969), Dennis Nineham, Warden of Keble College, Oxford, remarked:

> (At an investigation into current biblical interpretation initiated by the World Council of Churches some five years ago) I became increasingly aware of certain assumptions on the part of many of my colleagues, assumptions which were important because they largely accounted for the zest and sense of urgency they brought to their exegetical work. They assumed, first of all, that when they had discovered the meaning of a passage, they were dealing with a word of God, part of God's self-disclosure to the situation in which the words were originally written or spoken. But more than that, they at least started with the assumption that that word of God would also prove to have a contemporary meaning, and that the exegete's task was not completed till he had discovered what it was. To put the distinction in a rough and ready way, the exegete has

> not only to answer the question: What it *meant*, but also the question: What it *means* (pp. 180f.).

This he did not find to be self-evident. Many statements in ancient texts have no meaning at all today in any normal sense of the word. Nor does the Bible look to outward appearance like a book which has one single overall meaning or a single coherent body of truth: it is much more complex, much more fragile than that.

Now if these observations are near the mark, it becomes obvious that the whole question of 'biblical theology' will have to be completely rethought – and that they are indeed near the mark is indicated by supporting comments elsewhere. C. F. Evans, Professor of New Testament at King's College, London, has questioned the significance normally attached to the biblical canon in a paper entitled 'Scripture and Tradition' (*Religious Studies* 3, 1967):

> Is it, after all, so obvious that the Christian faith was meant to have a holy Scripture in the sense of the Old Testament, which it succeeded in demoting but fatally took as its model? Granted that the written text is strong precisely where tradition is weak, that as a fixed text it is less prone to corruption and more capable of acting as a purge, are these more than debating points, as good in their way as the debating points from the other side that it is the church which decides the canon and that Scripture does not interpret itself? Do they have to be blown up into a doctrine of holy authoritative Scripture (p. 336)?

The argument is taken further in 'Is Holy Scripture Christian?' (to be published, with other papers, by SCM Press, 1971; for background to the argument and further details see also John Bowden, *What about the Old Testament?*, and T. G. A. Baker, *What is the New Testament?*, SCM Press, 1969). As was mentioned in the Preface (p. 13), the *Reader* itself illustrates the confusion reigning over the use of the Bible in modern theology. If the new approach is taken seriously and developed further, it may be that a much-needed clarification of the principles for the use of the Bible in argument will emerge.

Now if the Bible is a difficult book, where else does the theologian turn? Is he to resort, rather, to tradition, and particularly tradition as it is to be found in the doctrines and confessions of the church? Just how much importance these doctrines have had in the past was indicated by Maurice Wiles, now Regius Professor of Divinity at Oxford, in his 1968 lecture, 'Looking into the Sun' (*Church Quarterly*, January 1969). He argued that biblical criticism could be accepted by the church in the nineteenth century and after because the church also possessed a basic outline of doctrine, related to the Scriptures but existing in its own right in practical independence of them. 'In the faith of Nicaea and of Chalcedon, belief in God the Father, the incarnation and saving work of the Son, the reality of the Holy Spirit's presence in Church and sacrament and Christian believer, the substance of the Church's faith seemed able to dwell secure and unscathed, whatever the scholars might discover in the course of their critical investigations of the Bible' (p. 192). His lecture goes on, however, to stress the need for criticizing this tradition as rigorously as the Bible itself: biblical criticism must be followed by doctrinal criticism.

Doctrinal criticism cannot be content with the traditional method of taking a particular doctrine (Nicaea, Chalcdeon) and contemporary thought about the world and then wrestling with the two until they can be shown to be compatible notions. Rather, doctrines, however venerable, are to be seen as historically conditioned interpretations, intimately bound up with the world-view of a bygone age. They are therefore no longer live options for man today; he is not in a position either to affirm them or deny them in the form in which they were originally presented. As the critic studies them he may, by recreating them in their context, find new meaning in them; but he may – as Nineham suggests in the passage quoted above – find that they are sometimes either meaningless, or even wrong.

How doctrinal criticism works out can be seen in Professor Wiles' book *The Development of Christian Doctrine* (CUP 1967), which outlines the arguments which led to the formation of the principal doctrines of the church and then criticizes them in that light. Perhaps the most thought-provoking of his writings, however, is his paper 'Does Christology rest on a Mistake?' (*Religious Studies* 6, 1970, pp. 69–76). This paper, too complex to be summarized briefly here, raises as important questions for the doctrine of the person of Jesus Christ as do the papers mentioned above for the Bible – and again, it puts a question mark against a good deal of modern continental theology.

These instances show just how far the critical questioning of the foundations of Christianity is being taken: nothing is exempt. Yet it would be wrong to gain the impression that the questioning is destructive. On the contrary, it seems a valuable attempt to remove religious belief from a strait-jacket and to do justice to the complex phenomenon that it can now be seen to be. Theology today has to be more open, more questioning; yet as it moves in this direction it also seems to be becoming more positive. If the theology of the early nineteen-sixties was predominantly negative and iconoclastic, the theology of the last two or three years has taken a more positive turn.

This development is exemplified by one of the best books of systematic theology to appear since the Second World War, John Austin Baker's *The Foolishness of God* (Darton, Longman and Todd, 1970). The author, who is Chaplain of Corpus Christi College, Oxford, is not afraid to develop a new natural theology against which to set his interpretation of human existence and the person of Jesus of Nazareth. On a smaller scale, John Hick's *Christianity at the Centre* (SCM Press, 1968), shows itself undaunted by philosophical attacks on Christian belief. Ronald Gregor Smith, who in his 1966 book *Secular Christianity* seemed to present a very negative view of Christian faith, underwent what to many readers was a startling change in the presentation of his thought in *The Doctrine of God* (Collins, 1970). 'Transcendence is what I must concentrate on!' was the remark that Professor Galloway, who prepared the manuscript for publication after Gregor Smith's death, consistently found in the latter's notes.

The examples could be multiplied. On the more technical side, John E. Smith's *Experience and God* (OUP, 1968) offers some important new lines of approach. Finally, however, it might be worth noting a discovery about the present trend of thought relating to theology that came as a pleasant surprise to the editors of the *Reader*. Between 1966 and 1970, circumstances kept them apart, and they met personally only once and corresponded hardly at all. One continued his work at Lancaster University and as visiting professor at Union Theological Seminary, New York; the other as Editor of SCM Press. Towards the end of 1969, each completed, quite independently, a book reflecting more recent reading: James Richmond, *Theology and Metaphysics* (SCM Press, 1970) is a philosophical study of a taut and well-polished kind; John Bowden, *Who is a Christian?* (SCM Press, 1970), is a more popular and hastily-written meditation on a wide range of literature, including books on science and the arts. In style and content the two works are very different, and they are based on different areas of reading and thinking, yet both in the end and at various points along the way seem to be outlining the same kind of picture. It is a picture of an open-ended theology, unable to be dogmatic at any one point, yet able to present a case because of the complex range of considerations to which it is able to appeal.

If it is accepted that the theologian attempts to draw an outline map, an interpretative scheme of the universe, taking in such diverse areas as religious experience, moral experience, human existence, history, nature, aesthetic experience, then – even in the modern situation – he may well find himself directed towards God. God will not be an observable within the map, a hitherto unnoticed or unexplored constituent of the world. Rather, the overall map, or picture, might be said to be such that without God it lacks coherence, meaning and completion; it points to God as origin, ground and goal; it is transparent to God and, upon prolonged contemplation in depth, reveals God as the ground and condition of our experience.

Theology, then, seems to be moving into an exciting, more confident and more encouraging phase. The possibilities for it are as good as they ever were. The question is, however, whether they will be taken up as they should be. And that is where the third point made in the last section applies, the need for theology to be related to action rather than being left in isolation. The last words of this book may, therefore, fittingly be the words of one of the greatest theologians of the early church, whose work is concerned with precisely this problem: 'If you know these things, blessed are you if you do them' (John 13.17).

INDEX OF NAMES

INDEX OF SUBJECTS